KT-404-369

he North *October 18, 1851* The Franklin Expedition: Return of the *A...*
...klin—Dr. Kane's Expedition *April 15, 1853* Sir John Franklin: Lady
...Discovery of the Frozen Bodies of Sir John Franklin and His Men, by D...
October 12, 1855 The Arctic Voyagers: What Dr. Kane Has Discovered *October 13, 1855* The Last of the
...8 A New Arctic Expedition Denounced *November 8, 1859* The New Arctic Expedition: Dr. Hayes' Proposed
...Two Scientific Expeditions to Be Made *October 31, 1868* The Northwest Passage: A New Exposition Proposed
...Pole *June 6, 1871* Reported German Discovery of an Open Polar Sea *October 28, 1871* A Daring Enterprise:
...he *Polari...* Compelled to Return to Greenland: Strikes a Snag and Springs a Leak *April 25, 1872* Germany and
...ish Arc... Expedition *October 28, 1876* Further Particulars of the Arctic and Discovery: The Impracticability
...ant Stru...le to Reach the North Pole *October 30, 1876* The Greenland Colony: Projects for Polar Exploration
...79 Arc... Ballooning: An Englishman's Plan *July 30, 1880* The Anglo-American Polar Expedition *December*
...d in Sm...h's Sound *September 14, 1883* Lieut. Greely's Peril *September 15, 1883* Can Greely Be Relieved:
...eely Re...ted Dead: What Nordensdkjould Learned from the Esquimeaux *September 23, 1883* Is Lieut. Greely
Decembe... 22, 1883 For the Relief of Greely: The British Government Tenders the Use of the Steamship *Alert*
...ut. Gre...y Rescued: Five of His Companions Also Saved *July 18, 1884* Horrors of Cape Sabine: Terrible Story
...Comrad...s *August 12, 1884* The Scientific Observations of the Greely Party—Glimpses of Its Daily Life and
...ks and ...aise Bananas *November 15, 1885* Told in an Arctic Diary: The Retreat from Fort Conger and Life on
...eenland...East Coast *September 18, 1895* Nansen's Arctic Travel: Siberian Report of His Discovery Confirmed
...to Rea...the North Pole by Airship *July 26, 1909* Cook Reports He Has Found the North Pole *September 2,*
...Septem... 7, 1909 Newspapers Call It the Most Remarkable Coincidence in History *September 7, 1909* By
...orth P...by Airplane *March 21, 1926* Amundsen's Airship Will Fly This Week on Way to the Pole *March 28,*
...nundse...opes to Fathom Arctic Mysteries *April 4, 1926* Amundsen Arrives at King's Bay Base for Flight to
...A...1929 Byrd Flies to North Pole and Back: Trip From Kings Bay in 15 Hrs., 51 Min.; Circles Top of
...6 ...essage Ever Received From the North Pole *May 12, 1926* *Norge* Sails Over Vast Ice Desert: Start
... Kr...World: *Norge* Explorers Discover New Territory at Rate of 5,000 Square Miles an Hour *May 13, 1926*
...tter...arch Expedition: Says He Will Fly to Assist If *Norge* Is Forced Down in Arctic Wilds *May 15, 1926*
...rge...Sent to the *Times* *May 16, 1926* Hail, the *Norge*! *May 16, 1926* Braving The Perils of the Arctic
...he Voyage to the North Pole Planned by Wilkins *March 30, 1929* Why the Sun Leaves the Polar Regions *May*
...Magnetic Changes *February 22, 1931* Byrd Gets Medal and French Honor: Honor to a Conqueror of the Air
...rive: Wilkins Starts for Davenport with Replacements for Submarine *July 12, 1931* Wilkins off to Pole Again
...kins Submarine to Be Sunk in Ocean *September 30, 1931* Greely, 88, Aids Plan for Arctic Voyage: Leader of
...for the Arctic: Icebreakers Carry Scientists to Take Leading Roles in Second International Polar Year *July 27,*
...*May 3, 1936* Soviet Maps Trip Undersea to Pole *December 28, 1937* Wilkins Gives Up Polar Trip *October*
...57–58 World Research: 23 Countries Agree to Share in Planned Geophysical Year *December 11, 1954* Arctic
...ntific Studies: Americans Living on Ocean Get Data for Geophysical Year *June 9, 1957* Arctic Is Key Strategic
...Sails Under the Pole and 1,830 Miles of Arctic Icecap in Pacific-to-Atlantic Passage *August 9, 1958* Soviet Is
...vy Submarines Set to Explore Arctic Basin *March 7, 1958* New Role for the Arctic: A Discussion of Region's

THE
NORTH
POLE
WAS HERE

A *New York Times* Book

THE NORTH POLE WAS HERE

One Man's Exploration of the Top of the World

ANDREW C. REVKIN

KINGFISHER

KINGFISHER

Kingfisher Publications Plc
New Penderel House
283–288 High Holborn
London WC1V 7HZ
www.kingfisherpub.com

First published by Kingfisher Publications Plc 2006
2 4 6 8 10 9 7 5 3 1
1TR/1205/PROSP/PICA(PICA)/130MA/C

ISBN-13: 978 0 7354 1329 9
ISBN-10: 0 7354 1329 9

Copyright © *The New York Times* 2006

Book design by Anthony Cutting
Additional design by Carol Ann Davis
Edited by Deirdre Langeland
Cover design by Mike Buckley
Photo research by Maggie Berkvist

Printed in China

BIRMINGHAM LIBRARIES
WALMLE
J919.8
09/06

All rights reserved. No part of this publication may be reproduced, stored
in a retrieval system or transmitted by any means, electronic, mechanical,
photocopying or otherwise, without the prior permission of the publisher.
A CIP catalogue record for this book is available from the British Library.

A note on the articles:
Articles from the archives of *The New York Times* appear throughout
this book. These articles have been edited to fit the format of the book.
Please refer to the original article for full text.

For my sons, Daniel and Jack

Contents

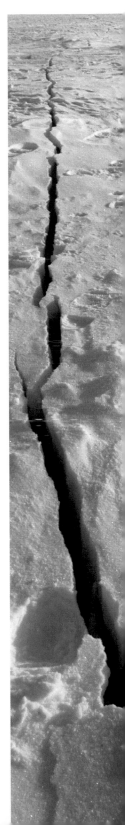

Chapter One

Where All Is

SOUTH

For nearly two hours, I have been staring out a small window on a droning propeller-driven airplane. The low, unsetting sun casts the plane's shadow off to the side, where it slides over what looks like an endless crinkled white landscape. But there is no land below us. There is only an ocean—a frozen one. We are flying out across a cap of floating, drifting ice that's the size of the United States. As far as the eye can see, colliding plates of ice raise jumbled miles-long ridges, some as high as houses. Here and there, the ice is split by cracks that expose the black depths of the Arctic Ocean underneath.

The plane is jammed with instruments and survival gear and scientists heading to the top of the world to study climate changes at the pole. Nearly five hundred miles ago, we left the most northern spot where people can live year-round, a Canadian military base called Alert, and headed farther north—as far north as you can go before you suddenly find yourself pointed south again.

Center image: The icecap at the North Pole is constantly shifting. On this flow forecast from December 30, 2004, arrows show the expected direction of movement, while the length of the arrow indicates speed.

Researchers have long been measuring a global warming trend, but it is in the Arctic that temperatures have risen the most. This research team is trying to understand why conditions are changing and what the changes may mean for people and the environment.

Finally, the pilot says we are nearing our destination. The plane's shadow grows as we descend. We are all overheated and sweating, stuffed into puffy layers of clothing and huge insulated boots. But no one else seems quite as nervous as I am about what is coming. In a few moments, the pilot is going to set this fifteen-ton rubber-tired airplane down on a rough runway scraped across the eight-foot-thick sea ice. The crew and scientists around me, who have done this for several years in a row, are munching peanut butter sandwiches and apples, reading books, chatting. I tighten my seatbelt. The Arctic has claimed the lives of many of the people who have been brave enough, or crazy enough, to press north. I wonder if the ice will hold, or if it will crack open and swallow the plane.

We finally touch down. There is a quick series of thumps and bumps and the rising roar of engines thrown into reverse. The propellers raise clouds of sparkling whiteness called "diamond dust"—crystals of flash-frozen sea mist far finer than snowflakes. A hatch opens and we climb down aluminum steps. Quite suddenly, I am standing on top of the world, about sixty miles from the spot around which the earth spins. The frigid air bites at my

cheeks. The bright sun forces me to squint. My boots scrunch on what feels like snow-covered ground. It takes a few moments before I remember I am walking on floating ice that is drifting about four hundred yards an hour over an ocean two miles deep—deep enough that ten Empire State Buildings could be stacked beneath us without breaking the surface. I am standing at the earth's last real edge, the last place where people cannot get very comfortable for very long.

Unlike the planet's South Pole—where a continent is home to permanent research stations and dozens of scientists, engineers, cooks, doctors, and other staff—at the North Pole nothing is permanent except the seabed far below. The ice that is here today will be somewhere else tomorrow. In a few years, much of what I am walking on, what our airplane landed on, will break up and slide out of the Arctic Ocean altogether through passages around Greenland, replaced by newly formed ice. A visitor once left a message in a container on the ice near this spot. It was found on a beach in Ireland a few years later.

Awaiting takeoff on an Arctic runway.

A thermometer registers Arctic temperatures of −15° Fahrenheit.

A couple of weeks ago, Russian workers flew here from Siberia to plow the runway into ice that had frozen solid through the long Arctic night. Six weeks after we leave, that same ice will pool with slushy meltwater and crack in pieces.

Welcome to life around the North Pole. The air is fifteen degrees below zero. The sun is circling in low, twenty-four-hour loops. If you define a day as the stretch between sunrise and sunset, today began on March 21 and will end on September 21. We are at one of the two places on the earth's surface where time loses all meaning. The only reason anyone here has any idea whether we should be asleep or eating lunch or breakfast is because the Russian crew running operations on the ice have set their watches to Moscow time. The only food I will eat in the next eight hours is a shared half-frozen salmon sandwich. And I am in love with this place.

This is a strange feeling for me. I never liked the cold much. When I was a kid, I was drawn to sun-baked regions, either real or imagined, preferring *The Swiss Family Robinson* to *White Fang*. I loved nothing more than pulling on a diving mask and snorkel in summertime to swim in warm bays and sneak up on fish and hermit crabs. I once spent more than a year on a sailboat journeying from the sunny South Pacific across the Indian Ocean and up the Red Sea.

Now I am at sea again, but this time I am standing on top of it. The sun is blinding, but the air is painfully cold. I feel like a mummy, stiffly stuffed into four layers of clothing. (I will end up smelling a bit like a

Since 2001, scientists have been camping on the floating ice a few dozen miles from the North Pole to study changes in the Arctic climate.

These South Korean trekkers were brought to the North Pole base camp by helicopter after they gave up on an attempt to ski there from Siberia. Behind them are the tents of Camp Borneo.

mummy, too, because we will not be able to wash for three days.) My toes tingle from the cold despite the giant insulated "bunny boots" I am wearing, but I am totally uninterested in fleeing to the small red tents nearby—the only hints of color in this blindingly bright ice world. I have somehow been captured by the magnetic pull of the Arctic, a tug that I have read about but never experienced.

For thousands of years, philosophers and navigators puzzled over what might be found at the world's northernmost spot. On one expedition after another, explorers died trying to reach this place. And now we have flown here in two hours from Canada.

Each year between mid-March and the end of April, after the single

Arctic day has dawned and before the ice gets too soggy, dozens of people come here—and not just scientists. There are tourists popping champagne corks, skydivers from Moscow, and ski trekkers from South Korea. There are extreme athletes from Manchester, England, who trained for their treks here by jogging around their neighborhoods dragging heavy truck tires from ropes tied around their waists. There are even marathon runners, including one man from Rhode Island who prepared for the first North Pole marathon, run here in 2003, by jogging in place in a dairy's walk-in ice cream freezer. Technology has invaded as well, and it helps make life here possible. We know our position within a few feet thanks to cell phone–size GPS navigational devices.

From the ice, I call my ninety-eight-year-old grandmother on a satellite telephone. She tells me she hopes I am wearing a hat.

Most visitors stay in a Russian-run base camp called Borneo, which is a strange mix of comforts and rugged simplicity. It has heated tents, electricity, a DVD player and TV, and four microwave ovens. But the toilet for men is nothing more than a waist-high igloo-style wall of ice blocks.

The scientists and I are using Camp Borneo only as a stepping-stone. Our final destination is an unnamed group of tents thirty miles closer to the pole—tents with no heaters, no DVDs, no champagne. The scientists are part of a small international army of dedicated researchers undertaking a host of inventive, and sometimes dangerous, projects aimed at understanding the changing face of the North Pole.

As I'm marveling at this frozen floating icescape, I am struck by the idea that later in this century the Arctic Ocean could well be uncloaked in the summer, no longer crusted in ice but instead mainly open water, as wave-tossed and blue as the Pacific and Atlantic oceans.

The global warming trend that raised the earth's average temperature one degree Fahrenheit in the twentieth century has had a stronger effect here. Average temperatures in some parts of the Arctic have risen as much as eight degrees since the 1970s. The sea-ice cover, which always shrinks a bit in summer, has for decades been pulling back more and more, exposing great stretches of open water. Computer simulations show that it may disappear altogether late in this century.

Most scientists have concluded that people are probably causing most of the recent global warming trend and some of the changes in the Arctic climate and ice by adding to the atmosphere long-lived gases that trap the sun's heat, somewhat as a greenhouse roof does. But, as always in science, questions follow answers. No one can be sure exactly how much of the recent warming is human-caused and how much is the result of natural fluctuations in the climate system. Indeed, there is little information on how temperatures in the high Arctic varied in centuries

past. Until recently, the forbidding nature of the vast icy seascape has prevented all but a few bold explorers from traveling here.

The planet has for millions of years seen great cycles of ice ages and warm periods. The changes under way around the North Pole could at least partly reflect natural flickers in climate, which is full of ups and downs.

But each year brings more signs that recent environmental shifts around the Arctic are extraordinary. Dragonflies are showing up for the first time in memory in Eskimo villages, causing children to run to their parents, scared of these unfamiliar insects. Robins are pecking at the tundra. The Arctic's native peoples have no name for this bird.

In a few decades, if the warming continues, it may also be harder to find a safe site to set up camp here. Perhaps there will come a time when the new North Pole will be a place that is easier to sail to than stand on.

In the meantime, though, the best option for studying the pole is to camp on the ice. Much science these days is done in laboratories, on computers, or using long-distance probes like orbiting satellites. But some science still must be done up close and personal. On this floating, shifting, melting ice, there is no place to stick a thermometer or other device and expect to find it again. So the team must come here, study the atmosphere, ice, and sea below, and return year after year to create a picture of what is going on.

The cap of sea ice on the Arctic Ocean has pulled back progressively in summers almost every year since 1978, when satellites started keeping track. A satellite image from 1979 (left) shows a larger icecap than an image from 2003 (right).

They call their project the North Pole Environmental Observatory, but that name gives the impression that it's some exotic domed facility. The reality is clear to me soon enough. After a quick ride in a Russian helicopter with black soot stains on its orange sides and a fabric strap holding the cargo doors shut, we arrive at the science camp. It consists of two tentlike huts, each about the size of a garden shed, and a scattering of buoys, tools, and boxes. At this spot, instruments recording sea currents and temperature were dropped to the sea floor one year ago on a two-mile-long line. Now they have to be retrieved from beneath that shifting ice. The procedure will require several of the researchers to get into diving suits and drop through a small opening melted through ice. And I thought that *I* was being adventurous.

To celebrate getting here, one scientist who arrived a couple of days before us, Jim Johnson, erected a red-and-white-striped barber pole and a sign that said NORTH POLE IS HERE.

But after a day or so, Johnson changed the wording, so that the sign now reads NORTH POLE WAS HERE.

The past tense is meant as a joke. The drift of the ice guarantees that anyone who is at the North Pole at one moment is not there a few minutes later.

But the sign also reflects the broader and much more profound idea that confronts everyone up here: that the unreachable, unchanging North Pole of our imagination, history, maps, and lore no longer exists.

The North Pole is a moving target, as a scientist's make-shift sign, at left, indicates.

From *The New York Times*

How to Get to the North Pole

BY ANDREW C. REVKIN

July 2003: My trip to the North Pole started with a car ride from my home in New York State to Newark, New Jersey. From Newark International Airport, I took a short evening flight to Ottawa, Canada, and then the fun began. On each leg of my trip, the planes and airports got smaller and the temperature colder. The runways switched from asphalt to packed snow.

A Boeing 737 carried me north to Iqaluit, the capital of Nunavut, Canada's newest territory. With some scientists and a reporter from the *Dallas Morning News*, Alexandra Witze, I boarded a twin-engine Beechcraft, which is the local equivalent of a Greyhound bus, stopping at ever-smaller outposts on the long route north until it reached the end of the line, Resolute.

Resolute lies on a winding passage through a maze of islands about nine hundred miles south of the pole, right near the place where the nineteenth-century British explorer Lord Franklin and his crew lost their way, went insane, and—dragging themselves over the frozen landscape—died.

After a night at the metal-roofed Narwhal Inn, it was time for the four-hour flight to the pole, including one last stop—at Alert, a Canadian military outpost and the northernmost place permanently occupied by people—to top off the fuel tanks.

Finally, four days and 2,900 miles from New York, the fifteen-ton plane lurched heavily as it landed on a runway carved by a Russian bulldozer on the drifting ice sixty miles from the pole.

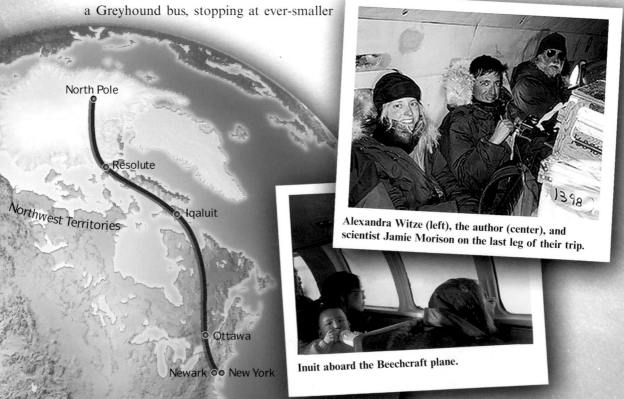

Alexandra Witze (left), the author (center), and scientist Jamie Morison on the last leg of their trip.

Inuit aboard the Beechcraft plane.

Refueling before take-off from Camp Borneo.

Jamie Morison (left)
and Tim Stanton check
equipment before
loading the plane.

From *The New York Times*

Reporting from the North Pole

BY ANDREW C. REVKIN

The North Pole, June 5, 2003: Notebook computers, digital cameras, and satellite telephones are enabling journalists to do what seemed impossible just a few years ago: transmit stories and images from the world's last untamed edges.

But technology still has limits, and they may be most obvious on the floating ice near the North Pole.

During my stay there, I learned the art of practicing journalism at fifteen degrees below zero.

First, the basics: Bring pencils, not pens. Ink freezes. Bring lots of pocket warmers, little yellow packets that heat up for hours when exposed to air. These are not just for fending off frostbite, but also for keeping your batteries warm.

And of course bring tape, every kind— electrical, duct, and the like—to fix the things that break (they will break) and to attach those pocket warmers to the back of a camera, the side of a microphone, the bottom of a laptop computer.

Satellite telephones have significant limitations. The signals travel in a straight line, so getting the antenna right is essential. There are sometimes painful gaps in conversations while the transmission jumps from one satellite to the next. Things can get tense if you are in the habit of watching the rise and fall of the little glowing bars on your laptop screen that show the data flow when you e-mail a big file. Halfway through the thirty- or forty-minute process of sending a picture, it is not uncommon to see the bars disappear altogether.

Despite the limitations, I am still amazed at the ability to link the last frontiers on a fast-shrinking planet.

The author files a story from base camp.

Alexandra Witze makes a call by satellite phone.

A scientist takes notes with a pencil. The ink in pens freezes at Arctic temperatures.

Chapter Two

The Imagined POLE

At one point during my stay on the sea ice, I pull on my fleece face mask and fur-collared parka and thin glove liners and thick outer gloves and air-filled white rubber boots and wander out of a tent at the Russian base camp. I walk about a quarter-mile away, far enough that the chugging of the electrical generators fades to windy silence. I kneel by the edge of a jagged opening in the ice where the giant floe we are camped on has split and the two halves are slowly pulling away from each other. New black ice is already forming on the exposed water, and remarkable tiny crystalline puffs called frost flowers have sprouted on that glassy surface.

The increasing pressures in the shifting ice plates create astonishing noises—low hoots, huffs, and ticks. There are quivering ripples on the open water, dancing to the ice vibrations. I am entranced by the stark beauty around me, from the ice dandelions to the dome of empty blue sky, until I am suddenly jerked back from the water by the camp manager, a bear-size man with a fur hat and booming voice. He says this is "too dangerous," explaining in broken English that a tourist fell into the twenty-eight-degree water the year before when a rim of ice like the one beneath me crumbled (the tourist was plucked to safety).

I back away, startled by my own carelessness. There is something deeply magnetic, even hypnotic, about the top of the world, and it is not just the force that tugs compass needles. There is something in human nature that seems to crave the edges of things, the places where the known, and the safe, ends.

Until the early 1900s, the regions around the North Pole remained little more than an idea to most of the human race. The exceptions were the native peoples of the Arctic, who were called Eskimos by outsiders but called themselves the Inuit, the Saami, and other names. For perhaps ten thousand years, they lived in isolation, scattered around the shores of the Arctic Ocean, harvesting the mammals and fish for fur and food, and surviving in incredible cold and long seasons of light and dark. But there is little evidence that even the Inuit, whose Arctic culture was most wedded to the sea, traveled far out onto the shifting sea ice toward the center of the Arctic Ocean—and why would they? The farther they went from land and open water, the less food they would find.

Starting more than two thousand years ago, adventurous explorers from Europe and Asia ventured north. Some sought mythical lands that

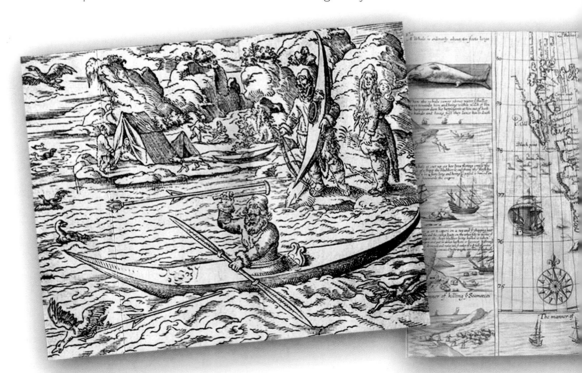

were said to be warm and inhabited by a happy race. Later, others searched for a theorized "open polar sea" beyond the great encircling barrier of Arctic ice. The idea that a warm, bountiful sea could be found at the top of the world was remarkably persistent, perhaps because no one could imagine a sea frozen to all horizons. More recently, adventurers have been coming here for thrills, a personal challenge, or to be first at something new, like running a marathon at the pole.

Many of the world's major civilizations, from China to India to Europe, had some ancient concept of a northernmost place, as well as a host of legends describing it, long before they had any evidence for what might actually lie there.

The concept of "north" started with navigation. As long as people have wandered wild frontiers and gone to sea, they have developed a sense of direction based on how the sun passes across the sky in a consistent way each day—between what we now call east and west—and how certain stars sit in predictable places at night. In the Northern Hemisphere, there is one star, Polaris, or the North Star, that sits relatively still in the sky even as the world does its daily spin around its axis. That star defined what people now

Left: A sixteenth-century rendition of an Inuk in a kayak. A whaling industry map from 1626 (center) and a page from Wright's 1598 *World Maps* (right) are decorated with fanciful renditions of the creatures thought to live in the Arctic.

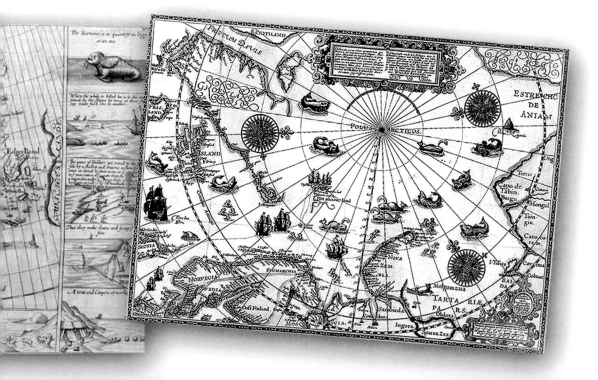

Top: A 1620 map of
the North Pole by
Gerardus Mercator.

think of as north long before there was a word for that direction. In fact, the word Arctic came from *Arktos*, the Greek word for "bear" and the name for a constellation, the Great Bear, that includes what is now called the Big Dipper and points to the North Star.

Long ago, philosophers began wondering about the land to the north and the mysterious star that seemed to lead to it. One ancient Hindu and Buddhist view of the world held that all the stars in the heavens were linked by ropes of wind to the North Star, which sat directly over a giant, unreachable mountain that was the center of the world. Around that center lay four landmasses separated by great flowing rivers.

Nearly three thousand years ago, Greek historians wrote of a society called the Hyperboreans, an immortal race of people who lived in happiness and warmth beyond the source of the North Wind. One of the first recorded instances of an explorer seeking to probe the mysteries of the world's northern regions was a voyage taken 2,300 or so years ago by a Greek explorer named Pytheas. His original writings no longer exist, but other historians referred to his descriptions of a journey he undertook in part to find what lay north of known countries in a region he called Ultima Thule (pronounced too-lee), the "most distant land." Pytheas clearly described places that appear to be the British Isles, as well as an island that is a six-day sail farther north (possibly Iceland) where the night was just three hours long. Beyond that place, he wrote, the sea was no longer liquid.

Around the time Pytheas was on his journey, the Chinese discovered

Spring

Sun

Summer
(N. Hemisphere)

Autumn

that a magnetized needle always pointed north. That method of way-finding rapidly spread around the world. Again, north was a special notion—a direction but not yet a destination.

Eventually, speculation began about the source of the pole's magnetic pull. Starting in the 1300s, some European texts spoke of a great magnetic mountain, described in some cases as thirty miles across, that accounted for the magnetism. Scientists now know that the planet's magnetic field has its northern pole around one thousand miles south of the geographic North Pole, over what is now Canadian territory. The magnetic northern pole is also moving, probably reflecting changes in the circulation of the planet's iron core. The magnetic field is generated deep in the earth as the molten iron core swirls with currents.

People in warmer parts of the world began to understand one characteristic of the North Pole (and the South Pole) long before they experienced it: that the ends of the earth have a single six-month stretch of daylight and a single night. The planet is a spinning sphere that circles the sun once a year. But it is tilted in its spin, so that each pole points slightly away from the sun for six months, in constant shadow, and faces the sun for the other six months, in constant daylight.

Still, all of this was grasped only in theory, and the North Pole remained a place of fantasy in the popular imagination. In a series of maps of the North Pole published in the late 1500s and early 1600s, the German-born geographer Gerardus Mercator brought together all of the tidbits of lore that had been passed down over the

Winter
(N. Hemisphere)

Bottom: During the Northern Hemisphere's summer, the earth is tilted with its North Pole toward the sun. As the earth rotates, areas farther south alternately face toward and away from the sun, creating periods of night and day, but the North Pole is in constant daylight for six months. In winter, the North Pole is tilted away from the sun, and stays in darkness for six months.

The HMS *Investigator* trapped in the ice during a voyage in search of the lost explorer Sir John Franklin.

centuries. His maps showed an ice-free open polar sea surrounded by four great islands, similar to the landscape envisioned in Hindu and Buddhist Asia thousands of years earlier. The maps included Lodestone Mountain, a mythical source of the earth's magnetism. In some cases, its pull was described as so powerful that it could carry a ship to its doom by tugging on the iron nails holding its planks together.

Right up through the 1800s, the ice-locked region around the North Pole remained a place that no one had seen, so fanciful notions persisted. Nineteen-year-old Mary Wollestonecraft Shelley, who in 1816 began writing the classic horror novel *Frankenstein*, had her great monster vanish by running north over the sea ice toward the pole after exacting its revenge on its creator. Santa Claus, who evolved from mingled European traditions of gift-giving saints and spirits and traveled on a reindeer-drawn sleigh as early as 1820, got his North Pole home in the 1860s in American poetry and artwork by the famed illustrator Thomas Nast.

What better place for a monster to vanish or for Santa to hide his workshop than a frozen spot beyond the reach of man?

One alluring theory that lasted through much of the nineteenth century held that the earth was hollow, with massive holes to its interior at the North and South Poles. According to this theory, the same tilt of the earth that casts the poles in darkness for half of the year would allow the interior of the earth—and the people who were imagined to live there—to experience two summers. The sunlight would shine through one or the other of the poles as they tilted toward the sun.

Though polar legends persisted, the isolation of the North Pole could not last. Global trade was expanding quickly in the 1800s, and countries were eager to find new sea routes. Ships and navigation methods were improving. The great wealth of England and other seafaring countries spawned an intense race for discovery and conquest at the top of the world.

But the Arctic did not give up its secrets easily.

From *The New York Times*

Will Compasses Point South?

BY WILLIAM J. BROAD

July 13, 2004: For thousands of years compasses have pointed navigators toward the North Pole, but the magnetic field that draws compass needles north is constantly moving and shifting—and may one day collapse entirely.

The collapse appears to have started in earnest about 150 years ago. The field's strength has waned 10 to 15 percent, and the deterioration has sped up recently, increasing debate over whether it means that a reversal of the lines of magnetic force that normally envelop the earth is near.

Deep inside the earth, the magnetic field arises as the fluid core oozes with hot currents of molten iron, and this mechanical energy gets converted into electromagnetism. During a reversal, the main field weakens, almost vanishes, then reappears with opposite polarity. Afterward, compass needles that normally point north would point south. The last one took place 780,000 years ago.

In theory, a reversal could have major effects because over the ages many aspects of nature and society have come to rely on the field's steadiness. It could knock out power grids, hurt astronauts and satellites, and confuse birds, fish, and migratory animals that rely on the steadiness of the magnetic field as a navigation aid.

In June 2004, the European Space Agency approved the world's largest effort at tracking the field's shifts. A trio of new satellites, called Swarm, will monitor the collapsing field and help scientists forecast its prospective state. No matter what the new findings, there is no reason to panic, scientists say. Even if a flip is imminent, it might take two thousand years to develop.

DISCOVERY OF THE NORTH POLE AND THE POLAR GULF SURROUNDING IT.

JOHN B. SHELDEN.

This nineteenth century painting, *Discovery of the North Pole and the Polar Gulf Surrounding It*, shows a mile-high iron cone at the top of the world, presumably the source of the pole's magnetism.

GEOGRAPHIC NORTH POLE

2001

1994

1984

1620

1600

1972

1760

1640

1962

1740

1680

1720

1948

1700

1780

1800

1820

1904

1840

1860

The magnetic pole is constantly moving. This map tracks its changing locations.

The aurora borealis, which is often visible during during the winter months in the Arctic, inspired many myths about the North Pole.

From *The New York Times*

The hollow earth theory held that an explorer could journey into the massive hole at the North Pole, travel through the center of the earth, and emerge at the South Pole. An article printed in The Times *described the theory in detail.*

The North Pole a Hole; Likewise the South

New York, April 4, 1908: The first public meeting of the Reed Hollow Earth Exploring club was held last night, and was attended by men and women interested in science and polar exploration. William Reed, founder of the club and exponent of the hollow earth theory, described the two poles as being in reality two openings, each a thousand miles wide.

All kinds of good things are to be had by those hardy explorers who reach the interior of the earth, including precious stones and metals, although, so far, all that have come out from those regions to the other world are icebergs, penguins, warm winds, and the aurora borealis.

In his lecture Mr. Reed said, "There is no reason to doubt that there are inhabitants living in the interior of the earth. The climate is warm, and they have the advantage of two Summers. When the sun is at the south pole it shines right through the great opening in the earth, which is fully a thousand miles wide. By the time the sun has got around to the north pole it can be seen through the opening at the other end, so that these people get two Summers and two Winters in their year. It would be just as easy to sail a boat around the crust of the interior of the earth as it would be on the outside.

"Icebergs found in the polar regions must come from somewhere, because they are frozen from fresh water." Mr. Reed continued. "I think they are formed at the mouths of the rivers in the interior of the earth, which do not get the full effect of the sun's rays shining through the center of the planet."

He hoped to get there and prove that his theories were correct.

An engraving from the early-nineteenth century depicts the aurora borealis blazing above the Arctic ice.

Chapter Three

Cold
REALITY

W

e are stranded. I am sitting in a barely heated blue-and-pink tent on the sea ice, with half-a-dozen tired, hungry scientists and other expedition members. We have been waiting four hours for a Russian helicopter to shuttle us several miles to the scientists' base camp, and we have just learned that it may be another four hours before it comes. There is no more helicopter fuel, and the next plane carrying fuel from Russia to the ice airstrip out here cannot fly because of a big storm over Siberia, six hundred miles away.

It is around this time that we share the crunchy, half-frozen salmon-salad sandwich that one of the scientists, Jamie Morison, was smart enough to slap together back in Resolute Bay, Canada, half a frozen ocean ago. I pull out a juice box, which now has the consistency of a Slushee.

Still stuffed into insulated gear, some of the more experienced team members turn sacks of clothing and supplies into giant pillows. They know that every scrap of sleep is precious in twenty-four-hour daylight and quickly slump into snoring naps. Beneath the plastic flooring, the ice has melted in the small circle of heat thrown by the old Russian stove in the center of the tent. This creates a sloshy depression that feels a little like a cold waterbed.

Previous page: In a nineteenth-century painting, explorers in search of Sir John Franklin drag their boats on sledges over the ice in northern Canada.

At the ends of the earth, patience is not just a virtue; it is vital if you want to avoid going crazy. Having a bit of extra food along for emergencies is also helpful—frozen salmon tastes pretty good when there is nothing else around and no prospect of a real meal. And we have it easy. Most of the European and American expeditions that pushed toward the pole or in pursuit of passages above North America and Europe starting more than five hundred years ago had to spend at least an entire winter, and sometimes two or even three, with their ships stuck in the grip of ice.

The first explorers who headed this way were surprised to find the ice closing in on their ships as winter settled in. Many

vessels were crushed and lives lost. The following waves of Arctic mariners began to plan for the winters, using ships designed to slide up out of the water as the ice closed in on all sides. But they faced another challenge. Crews had to wait through the darkness and boredom and aching cold until the sun rose and there was enough of a thaw to resume their journey six months later. Madness, mutiny, murder, and cannibalism were sometimes the result.

To pass the time and entertain those who are awake, I sing an old English ballad. I grew up with sea songs. My father was in the merchant marine, taking oil tankers around the Atlantic,

A sixteenth-century drawing of "England's famous discoverers" depicts Sir Hugh Willoughby to the right of the royal coat of arms.

and loved the lore surrounding man's experiences on the oceans. This song is about one of the famously unlucky Arctic explorers, Lord Franklin, who ventured north three times in the early 1800s and only returned twice.

With a hundred seamen he sailed away,
To the frozen ocean in the month of May.
Seeking a passage around the pole,
Where we poor sailors do sometimes go.

Lord Franklin, a British naval officer, was hardly the first to vanish with his entire team. In 1553, one of the first British explorers to head into the Arctic, Sir Hugh Willoughby, was part of a three-ship expedition seeking a route north over Russia. Winter arrived. His ship was separated from the others, which found safe havens. The following year, Russian fishermen came upon Willoughby's ship. Venturing aboard, according to one account, they found all sixty-three crew members frozen in place, "some of them seated in the act of writing, pen still in hand, and the paper before them; others at table, platters in hand and spoon in mouth."

Later, historians realized the crew had died of carbon monoxide poisoning after plugging up every possible air leak and vent. They kept out the deadly cold but kept in the invisible, odorless, and deadly gas coming from the coal burning in their stoves.

Over time, explorers began to learn from such disasters. In 1819, Lieutenant William Edward Parry of Britain, one of the first commanders of an Arctic expedition with the foresight to plan for a winter-long delay, arranged for a tentlike enclosure to be erected on the deck of one of the two ships he led. To break the monotony, the crews had orders to exercise on deck every twenty-four hours. They put on comic plays every other week with costumes brought along for that purpose. The officers taught the illiterate deck hands how to read and write. Parry played his violin.

Through the dark months, they printed a newspaper, the *North Georgia Gazette and Winter Chronicle*. It was a weekly collection of essays, poetry, and whatever else could possibly seem like news to sailors cooped up on vessels trapped in the ice.

In 1827, Parry undertook one of the first expeditions specifically aimed at reaching the North Pole. He fell far short, but by then had become a celebrity—the first Arctic star but hardly the last. In the nineteenth century and the first half of the twentieth century, those who sailed, hiked, sledded, or flew north were some of the world's most celebrated heroes. The isolation, mystery, and deadliness of this region added to the mystique surrounding those who survived their adventures here.

The first voyages north were mainly for practical reasons, to find new northerly shipping routes from the Atlantic Ocean that would allow ships to reach the Pacific without sailing south around Africa or South America. But the brutal conditions made the trips into extraordinary tests of courage and endurance.

Everyone who ventures out onto Arctic ice these days senses the tracks, or in some instances the ghosts, of those who first explored this place. As you fly with ease over frozen seas that swallowed so many ships and sailors, it is impossible not to feel awestruck about such efforts—even the failed ones, even those of the men who later lied about their achievements. And there were an awful lot who did so.

Jim Osse, a member of the team of scientists I am accompanying, is not the kind of person anyone would call timid. After all, his job up here will require him to put on diving gear and drop through a hole melted through the eight-foot-thick ice into the dark, seemingly bottomless ocean below. Still, he is in awe of those early expeditions. "You read those books when you're up here, about Peary and those guys, and it does kind of cheapen this experience," he tells me. "Twenty-four hours from Seattle, I'm on the Arctic icecap. Some people might think it's rather bold and daring, but these days all exploration is kind of forced, finding

Lady Jane Franklin
inspired forty
separate
expeditions in
search of her
missing husband.

things to create a challenge because living doesn't require much challenge."

The obstacles encountered by the early Arctic voyagers made for gripping news accounts and books. Often the public was more interested in the drama of the missions than it was in the goals of those braving the ice. The accounts of these men were stirring and often grisly. They described great wonders: ferocious swimming white bears, sea creatures with long single horns like a unicorn (narwhals) or great tusks (walruses), lands covered in high sheets of ice, skilled hunters who were comfortable in brutal cold and lived in huts built of ice blocks. They described horrors: toes and fingers blackened and amputated from frostbite; bleeding gums, sores, and teeth lost to scurvy; and worse. It often seemed impossible to survive, but they did.

For many of these Arctic adventurers, much of their celebrity came from simply making it home alive. Their actual accomplishments were often either very limited or exaggerated. In fact, despite a long history of claims of success, it would take until 1968 for anyone to prove he had reached the North Pole by any means other than an aircraft or submarine.

Lord Franklin was perhaps the most famous Arctic explorer of all. His first two trips, mainly overland in northernmost North America, earned him the nickname "the man who ate his boots" after he survived a grueling trek that killed most of his companions. But his fame really grew out of his disappearance, not his achievements. He left England in the spring of 1845 on a mission to find the Northwest Passage, the water route that was thought to connect the Atlantic and Pacific oceans across northern Canada. He departed with a crew of 134 aboard two sailing ships, the *Erebus* and the *Terror*. The reinforced ships had already successfully probed icy waters around Antarctica—they were fitted with steam engines and propellers that could be raised or lowered into the sea to help push through the ice. In late June some whalers in Baffin Bay, west of Greenland, spotted the ships tied to an iceberg. That was the last time they were seen by anyone other than the Inuit.

As the ballad explains:

Through cruel hardships they mainly strove,
Until their ship on mountains of ice was drove.
Only the Eskimo in his skin canoe,
He was the only one who ever came through.
In Baffin Bay where the whalefish blow,
The fate of Franklin no man may know,
The fate of Franklin no tongue can tell,
For there does Franklin and his good
crew and the fishes dwell.

His ill-fated expedition, which vanished after leaving England to great fanfare, was the first of many Arctic exploits and misadventures to capture international attention. From the *Times of London* to *The New York Daily Times*, newspapers were filled with stories of his disappearance and the subsequent search for survivors. They chronicled successful efforts by his wife, Lady Jane Franklin, to convince Britain and the United States to send out rescue expeditions seeking those who vanished. One after the other, ships put forth, trying to retrace Franklin's route.

Altogether, the quest for evidence of the lost Franklin expedition spurred the greatest burst of Arctic exploration of all. England and the United States sent out some forty expeditions between 1848 and 1859.

The disappearance of Lord Franklin set off one of the most active periods in Arctic exploration.

An 1859 portrait of
Elisha Kent Kane in
the cabin of his ship,
the *Advance*.

In the end, they did piece together, from a scattering of skeletons and fragments of clothing and ship's wares, the terrible ordeal suffered by the men in those ships. Historians concluded that the ships were abandoned after they were trapped and damaged by the ice in September 1846. The crew members hauled whatever they could carry over the ice to the barren shores of the glacier-cloaked islands fringing the top of North America. In notes left behind, they said Franklin died in June 1847, although the cause was not described. Survivors ventured south on foot, slowly dying off from starvation and lead poisoning from badly canned food. The last of them perished in a place now called Starvation Bay.

Another goal of Arctic explorers at that time was to discover whether the persistent legends about a warm open sea beyond the fringe of ice were true. It is hard to believe now, but in 1855, *The New York Times* ran on its front page a story reporting that an expedition by the American adventurer Elisha Kent Kane spied the long-sought "Open Polar Sea." Kane's book on that voyage sold almost as briskly as a Harry Potter novel sells now. He was a national hero, providing a vision of new frontiers to a divided country headed toward the Civil War. Kane's description of open seas, whether the result of a mirage or wishful thinking, helped spur more Arctic voyages. The romanticism surrounding such trips built steadily even as it became clearer over time that the Arctic Ocean was one of the earth's least romantic places.

At the end of the nineteenth century, though, the high Arctic's starkly frozen nature was completely revealed by Fridtjof Nansen, a Norwegian scientist and explorer. When Nansen learned that pieces of a ship crushed by the ice in the Arctic had drifted with the ice to the east coast of Greenland, he decided to do the same—except his boat would be built so that it couldn't be crushed. His expedition would literally "go with the floe." Leaving in 1893 from Norway, Nansen's ship drifted for three years with the icy currents from Siberia toward Greenland.

While his team didn't quite get there, they reached farther north than anyone had before, and their scientific observations are still cited by scientists today.

After Nansen's return, it was clear that the North Pole was the only remaining Arctic prize. Now most of those heading north appeared to be motivated mainly by fame and celebrity, not by the desire for new knowledge or practical rewards like shipping routes.

Magazines and newspapers, including *Harper's Magazine* and *The New York Times*, got caught up in the star power of the Arctic heroes, offering payments in return for exclusive rights to publish their stories. And the explorers, in turn, got caught up in the need to feed the public desire for heroism, even when the Arctic denied them the North Pole.

Polar Stars

The frenzy peaked in 1909, when two men separately claimed that they had reached the North Pole by dogsled.

On September 1 that year, Dr. Frederick A. Cook, an American physician and seasoned mountaineer and polar adventurer, showed up in Europe after two years in the Arctic and announced that he had reached the North Pole on April 1, 1908. Just four days later, a long-anticipated message was wired via Labrador in far northern Canada by the American navy commander Robert E. Peary, another veteran Arctic trekker, stating that he had planted the Stars and Stripes at the pole on April 6, 1909. Cook was being toasted at a banquet in Copenhagen with a garland of roses draped around his neck when the news about Peary's claim swept the hall. Cook publicly congratulated the man he considered second at the North Pole.

As Peary made his way back from what was his eighth Arctic effort, reporters told him about Cook's claim. He was furious. Peary had spent his life pursuing fame. As a young man, he had written to his mother, "I wish to acquire a name which shall be an 'open sesame' to circles of

Robert Peary with a team of dogs, returning from the Arctic aboard the *Roosevelt* in 1909.

Peary's longtime aide, Matthew Henson, the first African American to explore the Arctic.

culture and refinement anywhere." Now the ultimate prize seemed to have been snatched from his grasp.

Peary and his longtime aide, Matthew Henson, the first African American to explore the Arctic, said they saw no sign of anything left behind by Cook and his two Eskimo companions. Cook quickly countered that the shifting ice and the passage of a year between the two visits would have made it impossible for any evidence to remain at the pole.

Cook had been the expedition doctor on several of Peary's earlier Arctic forays, setting the bones in Peary's badly broken leg on one trip. But from that September on, and for decades to come, the two men and their camps of defenders battled over their competing claims of being first at the top of the world.

Cook was more at home with Eskimos and ice than the spotlight and celebrity, so he generally got the worst of it. He was quickly discredited in most circles after facing harsh attacks in the press from Peary and his supporters. Peary, in contrast, knew two U.S. presidents and was comfortable in high society. His case was strongly favored by the National Geographic Society, which supported his expedition, and *The New York Times*, which had loaned Peary $4,000 in return for exclusive access to his story (the equivalent of about $92,000 in 2005).

While the public followed the claims and counterclaims with the same intensity that now surrounds celebrity trials, scientists tended to discount the whole Cook-Peary fight from the start. On September 8, 1909, for example, even as the tempest over the polar claims built, a physicist from Cornell, Dr. John S. Shearer, told *The Times* that the exploits, even if proved, were mainly a stunt and would have value only to "vaudeville science."

Through the first two-thirds of the twentieth century, almost everyone else who attempted to reach the pole recognized that the shifting sea ice was a brutal barrier. So the next generation of Arctic pioneers tried to get to the top of the world either by flying over the ice or traveling beneath it.

Richard Byrd with a sextant during a preflight test.

The massive airship *Norge* stopped in England before its flight over the North Pole in 1926.

The next most celebrated attempt was a flight toward the North Pole on May 9, 1926, by two Americans, Richard E. Byrd and his pilot, Floyd Bennett. Decades later, historians proved that this flight never came close to the goal, although it vaulted Byrd to fame.

In the end, the first people to fly over the pole and prove it were Umberto Nobile, an Italian aviation engineer, Roald Amundsen, a renowned polar explorer from Norway, and Lincoln Ellsworth, a wealthy American adventurer. Three days after Byrd's flight, they floated north from Norway in a hydrogen-filled airship, the *Norge*, which Nobile had designed. Unlike Byrd's flight, which quickly came under fire from aviation experts, their passage over the pole was carefully documented. They flew on to Alaska, marking the first time anyone had flown entirely across the Arctic Ocean.

Submarines were the other logical choice for reaching a spot that sat in the middle of an ocean with an impassable crust of ice. The first attempt was made by Sir Hubert Wilkins, an Australian adventurer. He had already flown in 1927 over a different "pole" in the Arctic, a spot called the "Pole of Inaccessibility"—the place farthest from land in every direction. In 1931 he headed toward the geographic North Pole using a submarine on loan from the U.S. Navy and built before World War I. The sub, given the name *Nautilus* after Captain Nemo's vessel in the Jules Verne novel *20,000 Leagues Under the Sea*, reached the edge of the polar icecap and took measurements of sea temperature and water depth. But just before a dive beneath the ice, the captain discovered that the rudders used to submerge the vessel had been

Hubert Wilkins ca. 1931.

The American
submarine USS
Connecticut breaks
through the ice on an
Arctic run.

removed, perhaps as an act of sabotage by someone on the crew who
feared the under-ice mission.

One shallow dive was attempted, and on the way back to port the
Nautilus was so badly damaged in a storm that it had to be intentionally
sunk in a Norwegian bay.

After World War II, growing tensions between the communist Soviet
Union and the United States, on opposite sides of the Arctic Ocean,
made that frozen basin one of the first silent battlefields in what came
to be called the cold war. The Soviets had started setting up year-round
"ice stations" on the frozen icecap as far back as the 1930s.

On May 3, 1952, an American airplane landed at the pole. Its crew, U.S.
Air Force Lieutenant Colonel Joseph O. Fletcher and Lieutenant William P.
Benedict, became the first documented visitors to set foot on the ice there.

In August 1958, another ship named for Captain Nemo's vessel, a
nuclear-powered American submarine called the USS *Nautilus*, finally
achieved what Hubert Wilkins failed to do twenty-seven years earlier—
it cruised silently beneath the North Pole sea ice. Six months later, on
March 17, 1959, another nuclear sub, the USS *Skate*, surfaced through
a relatively thin plate of sea ice at the pole. The crew held a memorial

service in honor of Sir Hubert, who had been knighted in Britain for his exploits, and scattered his ashes at the spot he never reached.

But the submarine trips were not joy rides or pilgrimages. They were serious military missions, testing a way to carry nuclear-tipped missiles closer to the Soviet Union. The Arctic Ocean, so hostile to surface travelers, turned out to be a perfect place for submarines to lurk undetectably under the ice and surface to launch their deadly cargo. They also collected the first measurements of the thickness of the sea ice as they glided beneath it, and this data would eventually help scientists show that the ice was growing thinner.

Ten years later, on April 19, 1968, a team of four men finally succeeded where so many others had failed. Ralph Plaisted, an adventure-seeking insurance salesman from St. Paul, Minnesota, led three other men on a forty-four-day journey from northernmost Canada to the North Pole across the sea ice. They traveled in a decidedly unglamorous way, on Ski-Doo snowmobiles. By then, the excitement surrounding past polar treks had clearly faded. Instead of appearing under a front-page headline, the short *New York Times* story on their achievement ran on page 68.

From *The New York Times*

Who Reached the North Pole First?

BY WARREN E. LEARY

February 17, 1997: It has been a question debated in the annals of exploration for almost ninety years. Who was the first man to reach the North Pole, Admiral Robert E. Peary or Dr. Frederick A. Cook? The answer may be neither of the above.

Robert M. Bryce, a historical researcher who spent twenty years studying the great polar controversy, says evidence gleaned from the journals and diaries of the explorers themselves, as well as unpublished papers and accounts of companions and others involved in the Arctic expeditions, proves that neither man actually stood at the top of the world, though each man claimed he had.

The expedition papers of both men show that they made genuine attempts to reach the pole by dogsled in 1908 and 1909, he said, but were thwarted by harsh Arctic conditions, like the moving ice packs on which they were forced to travel, as well as limitations of the navigational instruments of the time.

"Perhaps no one could have reached the true pole at that time, with the massive amounts of supplies that would have been needed, the instruments of the day, and the conditions they encountered," Bryce said in an interview. "But neither man was willing to admit failure. So much was at stake."

Bryce, a librarian and document preservation expert, said his long interest in the controversy led him to begin work eight years ago on a Cook biography.

Bryce said he started out hoping to find evidence supporting Cook's claim. He said he felt Peary, whom he described as aloof, cold, and manipulative, and his influential backers had been unfair to the more personable Cook. "I wanted Dr. Cook to win," he said. "Who would want Peary to win? He was so unlikable."

But his book did not prove that Cook reached the pole first. In examining the explorer's journals and letters, Bryce found evidence that Cook had erased and doctored entries. Cook apparently was adjusting dates to match purported observations, Bryce said, including the claimed sightings of Arctic landmasses that do not exist.

If neither Peary nor Cook made it to the pole, then the first person to actually set foot there was Joseph Fletcher, who stepped off an Air Force C-47 plane that landed at the pole in 1952.

Dr. Frederick Cook rests on a dogsled.

Byrd (left) and Floyd Bennett board their plane, the *Josephine Ford*.

From *The New York Times*

Did Byrd Reach the North Pole?

BY JOHN NOBLE WILFORD

May 9, 1996: Seventy years ago, on May 9, 1926, in a decade notable for pioneering aviation exploits, Richard E. Byrd and his pilot-mechanic, Floyd Bennett, won fame as the first to fly an airplane to the North Pole. Or so they claimed. Doubts that they reached the pole have persisted to this day.

Now archivists at Ohio State University have found the diary Byrd kept on the flight. Most of the diary entries consist of Byrd's notes to the pilot, Bennett. The engine noise inside the cabin made it impossible to communicate by talking. Byrd would write questions, and Bennett would respond with written answers.

After a meticulous examination of the diary's contents, including some erasures at critical points, Dennis Rawlins, an independent scholar who specializes in analyzing the records of polar explorers, concluded that Lieutenant Commander (later Rear Admiral) Byrd almost certainly fell short of his polar destination and must have known at the time that he had not succeeded.

Byrd's airplane, a tri-motor Fokker monoplane named *Josephine Ford*, probably came within two and a quarter degrees of the pole before the two men, concerned about an engine leak, decided to turn back. That would have put the plane some 150 miles short, nearly close enough to see the top of the world.

If Byrd did not succeed, historians of polar exploration said, the team aboard the dirigible *Norge* should be recognized as the first to fly over the North Pole. Their flight occurred three days later than Byrd's, and its success in reaching the pole has never been questioned in light of the many precise navigational fixes taken by the crew.

Richard Byrd returns to a hero's welcome in New York in 1926.

Chapter Four

The Polar
PUZZLE

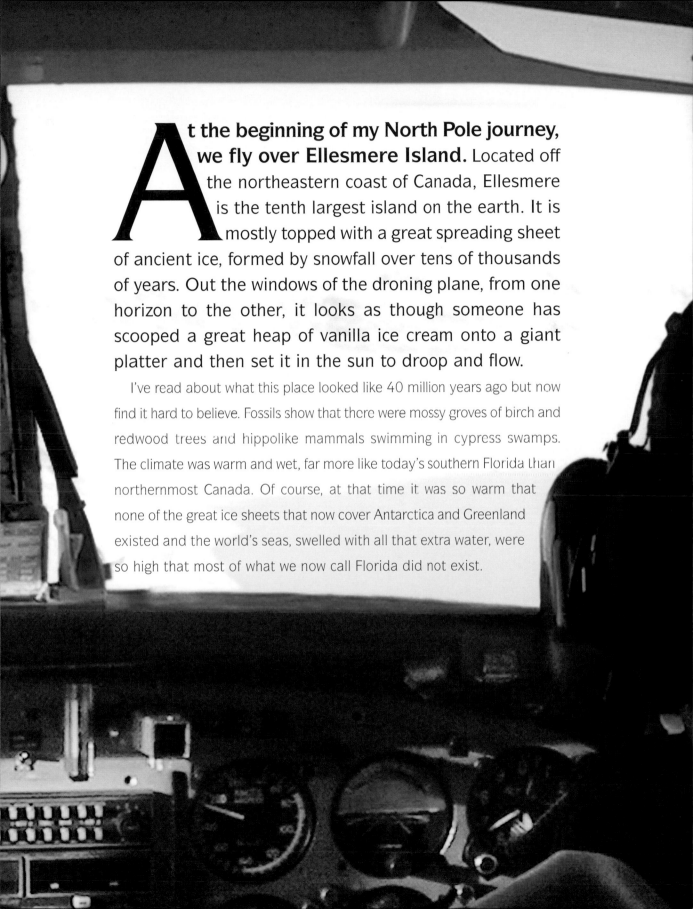

At the beginning of my North Pole journey, we fly over Ellesmere Island. Located off the northeastern coast of Canada, Ellesmere is the tenth largest island on the earth. It is mostly topped with a great spreading sheet of ancient ice, formed by snowfall over tens of thousands of years. Out the windows of the droning plane, from one horizon to the other, it looks as though someone has scooped a great heap of vanilla ice cream onto a giant platter and then set it in the sun to droop and flow.

I've read about what this place looked like 40 million years ago but now find it hard to believe. Fossils show that there were mossy groves of birch and redwood trees and hippolike mammals swimming in cypress swamps. The climate was warm and wet, far more like today's southern Florida than northernmost Canada. Of course, at that time it was so warm that none of the great ice sheets that now cover Antarctica and Greenland existed and the world's seas, swelled with all that extra water, were so high that most of what we now call Florida did not exist.

The great frozen plains sliding beneath our aircraft are a reminder that the earth's climate is always changing. In fact, over the last two million years, the earth has plunged into the deep cold of ice ages more than twenty times. These periods of cold lasted for tens of thousands of years at a time. The warm periods, like the last ten thousand years, have been the exception. The cooling and warming cycle seems to follow rhythmic variations in the way the earth orbits the sun. Climate experts say another ice age could come in ten or twenty millenniums but could also be delayed indefinitely as long as human societies keep pumping greenhouse gases into the atmosphere. The heat-trapping power of the gases is greater than the slight warming and cooling accompanying the shifts in the earth's orbit.

One of the biggest concerns of many climate experts is that in just one hundred years the ongoing buildup of the greenhouse gases could take us beyond the stable range of warmth that has been typical throughout that ten-thousand-year span in which all modern civilizations arose. The pace of change is a big part of the problem, along with the warming itself. Wildlife and farmers and water supplies can adapt to slow climate shifts but perhaps not to quick ones.

The Arctic has long been a valuable place to look for hidden pieces to the puzzle of past climate ups and downs, some of which are recorded precisely in the depths of glaciers like those on Ellesmere. The layers of snow, laid down year by year, century by century, contain bubbles of air and other substances that provide a record of past climates and atmospheric conditions.

The top of the world has attracted even more scientific attention recently. Even as it is providing clues that reveal past changes, the region itself is now exhibiting some of the most dramatic shifts in climate seen anywhere on earth.

Up here, scientific evidence has never been gained easily. But that has not stopped intrepid scientists from seeking it. Largely lost amid all

Previous page: Ellesmere Island looms through the windshield as the author flies over the Arctic.

Forty million years ago, the shores fringing the Arctic Ocean were covered with thick swampy forests of redwood and birch, like these in California.

After an Arctic journey in 1874, Karl Weyprecht (right), an Austrian explorer and physicist, convinced eleven countries to team up in a vast study of the far north. The map shows the location of International Polar Year stations, ringing the Arctic.

the adventuring, stunts, and competitive Arctic treks in the last two centuries, many serious scientific efforts to solve the riddles locked in the polar ice have been made. Even with all of the exaggerations and outright lies told about exploits in this icy realm, there is one truth: the extremes of the North Pole seem to inspire people, including scientists, to go beyond what others thought was possible.

Perhaps the most remarkable scientific effort of all was one of the first: the International Polar Year of 1882–83. This revolutionary effort to understand the remarkable conditions at the top of the world probed everything from the brutal weather to the magnetic fields, from the frozen ocean to the shimmering aurora borealis, or northern lights.

Nearly a century before the first spacecraft offered humans a wide-angle view of their home planet, the International Polar Year attempted to look at the big picture by setting up a network of research stations all around the Arctic. The stations had no way to stay in touch with one

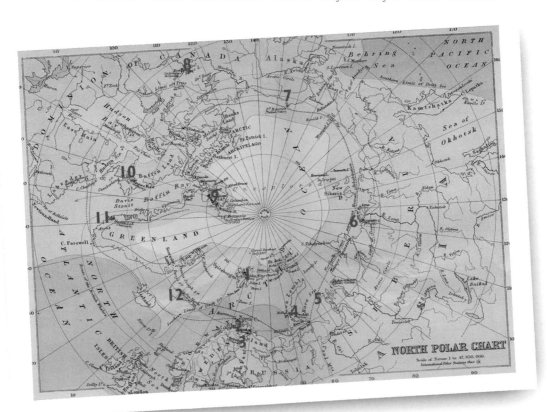

another—they collected data in isolation from the outside world month after month. But the instruments and recording methods at each station were coordinated, so that once the project was done, scientists could compile all the information and create the first snapshot of the remote region. A smaller effort was made at the other end of the planet, in areas near Antarctica.

Until that time, all of the probing in the Arctic was somewhat like a bunch of people working separately to assemble a jigsaw puzzle. Each person would collect some scattered pieces and try to fit them together. But no one shared information, and so nobody saw the big picture.

The Polar Year project grew out of the ideas of Karl Weyprecht, an Austrian explorer and physicist. After completing an expedition in the Arctic in 1874, he traveled from one scientific organization to another, urging them to create a unified research mission. He said the only way to understand Arctic patterns would be to monitor winds, snow, ice, temperature, and other conditions at many spots simultaneously and share the data. The international push into the Arctic until then, he said, had amounted to little more than a dangerous contest. As he wrote: "Immense sums were being spent and much hardship endured for the privilege of placing names in different languages on ice-covered promontories, but where the increase in human knowledge played a very secondary role."

Weyprecht died the year before the project got under way, but he is now recognized as having inspired a great moment in science: the first time some portion of the earth was probed by researchers from many countries and disciplines in the pursuit of shared knowledge. Altogether, eleven countries established fourteen stations around the Arctic. The effort was filled with difficulties and danger. An American expedition sent twenty-five men into the Arctic to collect data in 1881, but three years later only six returned. Among the survivors was the expedition leader, Adolphus Greely, who was initially criticized for his leadership. Rumors spread that the few survivors were in such dire straits that they survived only by eating the flesh of fallen comrades. But an investigation determined that Greely had not acted improperly.

The data collected through this project were significant, but more important was the change the first Polar Year marked in the way scientists work. Dr. E. Fred Roots, a leading polar scientist in Canada, wrote that from that time on, science would no longer be "an exclusive or elitist pursuit, often jealously guarded for reasons of national or institutional prestige." Instead, he said, "science developed into an open activity, in which everyone qualified could take part and in which the results belonged to the whole world and the quality of the science was judged by criticisms of other knowledgeable scientists, not by patrons or clients."

Similar coordinated explorations of the earth's remotest regions and oceans took place in the 1920s and 1950s, and another International Polar Year is planned for 2007–8, in hopes of providing a fresh snapshot of the recent changes in the Arctic.

Much has been learned, but there are still huge gaps in our knowledge about the North Pole and the ocean beneath it. Recently, I visited some polar geographers at the University of New Hampshire who spend summers on icebreaking ships, using electronic depth sounders to chart the mostly unmapped sea floor. Dr. Larry Mayer, the director of the Center for Coastal and Ocean Mapping there, used a computer to take me on a three-dimensional tour of the Arctic Ocean's vast basin. Through images projected on a wall, we traveled over the seabed, which was defined by a grid of lines where navy submarines and a few ships had passed through the area and taken depth readings.

Then he pushed a button, adding depth data from a new cruise they had just made in 2003. Suddenly a giant underwater mountain sprouted

where the old chart had shown a flat bottom. The mountain rose more than 9,000 feet from the sea bottom toward the surface. One of the old depth-sounding voyages had passed within a few miles but had completely missed it. "That's the state of our knowledge," he told me.

But the most profound gaps in scientific knowledge today are not about the shape of the Arctic seabed. They concern the region's past and future. A big discovery about one of the warmest periods in Arctic history was just made in 2004. That summer, three icebreaking ships full of scientists punched north into the ice-covered Arctic Ocean, trying to go back in time. They had no time machine, just a drill that could be lowered to the top of an underwater mountain range nearly a mile down.

For decades, cylinder-shaped cores of layered ancient rock and mud, about as thick as the barrel of a baseball bat, have been extracted from

Survivors of the Greely party with their rescuers. The five survivors are seated at front; Adolphus Greely is behind them in the center.

Scientists examine cylindrical samples of rock and mud pulled from the Arctic seabed 150 miles from the North Pole.

sea floors and lake beds around the world, providing the geological equivalent of a history book. Over millions of years, algae and tiny plankton in the water die and sink, mingling with silt and anything else carried in the water. The mixture eventually forms layers on the bottom that hint at what conditions were like at particular times in the past. Core drilling cuts through those layers, providing scientists with a bit of each. By analyzing the types of plants found, scientists can determine whether the water was fresh or salty like today's ocean. The composition of the microscopic shells of plankton can also reveal what conditions were like when they were formed. For example, past sea temperatures can be determined by looking at subtle variations in the chemistry of the shells.

But in the brutal conditions atop the Arctic Ocean, where sea ice slabs constantly grind, no one had ever been able to keep a ship in one spot long enough to drill a deep hole (and thus a hole that reaches far back in time). No one knew if it could even be done. Still, the $12.5 million project involving scientists from ten countries went ahead, adding to the long history of pioneering scientific research in the brutal conditions that are normal at the ends of the earth. From mid-August through early September, two icebreakers ran interference for the vessel with the drilling rig on its deck, trying to fend off the thickest floes so the drillers could remain motionless.

And it worked. In the midst of all of those shifting frozen slabs, one of the icebreakers, equipped with a nine-story-tall drilling rig, pulled dozens of fifteen-foot-long cylinders of mud and rock from five separate holes cut into the sea floor. When examined side by side back in a laboratory in Bremen, Germany, those cylinders of mud produced a record descending more than one thousand feet down through the sea floor and 57 million years back in time. And all of this was done just 150 miles from the North Pole.

In the fall of 2004, dozens of scientists from around the world met

to help read this muddy history book. Slices and samples were sent to other specialized laboratories set up to look at microscopic fossils, the chemistry of the mud, or other features that might reveal clues about the past. There were big gaps in the record, but there were still great discoveries to be made. The cores indicated that about forty-nine million years ago, while those hippolike creatures were wallowing in Ellesmere's swamps, the surface waters of the Arctic Ocean were so warm and fresh that they were covered with a kind of tiny fern called *Azolla*, which is a relative of the duckweed that coats many suburban ponds today. The researchers calculated that the temperature of the water was probably sixty-eight degrees in places where it now rarely rises above thirty-four degrees.

The cores also held hints about when the Arctic Ocean was cloaked with ice in past eras. The scientists were able to figure this out by looking for another kind of evidence in the sea floor: pebbles. In the great basin of the Arctic Ocean, much of the ice lasts for years before it either drifts past Greenland into the Atlantic Ocean or melts. Some Arctic ice forms along gravelly shorelines where pebbles and other debris get stuck in the ice. When the ice drifts back out toward the deep center of the ocean and melts, those pebbles rain down onto the seabed. They end up buried under the endless slow rain of silt and algae and plankton. Because they drilled their core on the peak of a mountain ridge, the researchers knew that there was no other way the pebbles could have gotten there. Even a strong current could not sweep such pebbles up the sides of the ridge. So layers with pebbles could only have formed when the Arctic Ocean had a cloak of ice. And layers without pebbles were likely created when there was no ice.

Their initial analysis of the cores implies that the last time the Arctic

Left: Modern *Azolla* ferns are similar to the ones that once covered the Arctic Ocean.

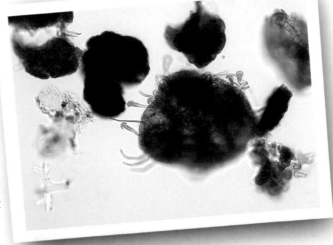

Azolla spores were found in the core samples, indicating that the Arctic Ocean was once warm and fresh.

Ocean was routinely free of sea ice was at least fifteen million years ago—and possibly much, much longer.

The scientists working on the drilling project were concerned that the Arctic might be poised to return to ice-free conditions that had not been seen in such a very long time—not just beyond human history, but back before humans first appeared as a species. A change of that size would be bound to come with surprises, and many of them would doubtless be unpleasant ones. Species adapted to current conditions could be imperiled, among them polar bears.

No one expects ferns to cover the polar sea anytime soon. But some experts doing the drilling work said that there was an important message in the patterns of change seen in the layered ancient mud, silt, and rock. Dr. Henk Brinkhuis, a Dutch geologist on the project, explained the Arctic pattern to me: warming reduces the ice that covers the ocean. This means that energy from the sun that would normally bounce off the bright surface of the ice is absorbed by the dark sea and land. In other words, a little warming causes a lot more warming. "You can get a really strong cascade," he said. And once it starts, it can take thousands of years to reverse.

There is much more to learn about the changes under way in the Arctic now. The 2004 expedition returned with just one set of samples from one spot in an ocean bigger than the United States. It will take many more data-gathering trips over many more summers before scientists can create a complete picture of the changes happening at the North Pole. As that picture becomes clearer and clearer, scientists are hoping to answer the question that is one of the largest pieces of the polar puzzle: are the recent warming and melting being caused by rising levels of heat-trapping gases flowing from factory smokestacks and car tailpipes around the world?

Many scientists say there is ample evidence pointing to a link. But the Arctic has seen great swings in temperature that were the result of natural changes as well, and humans have just begun to probe the puzzle.

The *Vidar Viking*, one of three ships that participated in an expedition to collect core samples from the floor of the Arctic Ocean.

ALASKA

RUSSIA

East Siberian Sea

CANADA

Chukchi
Borderland

Laptev Sea

Lomonosov
Ridge

Kara Sea

Gakkel
Ridge

Barents Sea

GREENLAND

A map shows the Arctic basin
(center) bisected by the
Lomonosov Ridge. The Gakkel
Ridge is slightly to the south.

FINLAN

ICELAND

NORWAY

From *The New York Times*

Fiery Secrets in the Arctic Depths

BY ANDREW C. REVKIN

July 1, 2003: Deep beneath the ice-sheathed Arctic Ocean, a thousand-mile seam in the earth's rocky crust, long thought to be dormant, has been revealed as a simmering necklace of volcanoes and hot-water vents that may harbor unique life forms.

The seam, which is called the Gakkel Ridge and bisects the polar ocean from Greenland to Siberia, is the least active of the midocean ridges found throughout the world's seas. These are the gutter-shaped valley and mountain systems where the crust of the sea floor spreads out to each side and hot magma pushes to the surface.

Earlier surveys measuring the magnetic signature of rocks in the Gakkel Ridge found that it generally spreads only a quarter-inch or so a year in each direction, about a seventh or less of the spreading rate seen in most midocean ridges. The slow spreading rate was presumed until now to prevent the surge of magma, the researchers and other experts said.

The likelihood of finding volcanoes and life-sustaining vents was so low that a thirty-member team that went to sea in the summer of 2001 to investigate the ridge included just one vent specialist, Dr. Henrietta N. Edmonds, a geochemist from the University of Texas.

"I was brought along as a funky add-on," she said. "They were saying, 'Man, she's going to be bored for a couple of months.'"

That was before the results started pouring in from her instruments, which were attached to cables as the team lowered rock-sampling dredges and checked hints of any upstream plume of mineral-rich, volcanically heated water gushing from the seabed into the frigid sea.

The researchers were shocked when more than 80 percent of the instrument readings detected warm water plumes over the six-hundred-mile portion of the ridge that was surveyed.

Some of the volcanic domes that the survey detected rise more than a mile from the three-mile-deep bottom of the rift valley running down the center of the Gakkel Ridge. The hot spots found along the ridge appear to have existed fairly consistently for as many as 25 million years in some cases.

The Gakkel's hydrothermal vents are similar to others found elsewhere in the world's oceans, most of them nourishing specialized ecosystems.

But because landmasses and deep-sea ridges separate the Arctic Ocean from the Pacific and Atlantic, it is possible that vents there—isolated for millions of years—might support species not seen anywhere else.

From *The New York Times*

Is There Oil Under All That Ice?

BY ANDREW C. REVKIN

November 30, 2004: Some of the scientists who examined the cores collected near the North Pole say that the seabed may hold oil and gas deposits.

Petroleum deposits were already charted along the shallow shelves fringing the Arctic from the North Slope of Alaska to northernmost Europe. But the cylinders of dark, ancient rock extracted from the Lomonosov Ridge, a submerged mountain range, were the first hint that such deposits may lie in the two-mile-deep basins near the top of the world.

The cores provided evidence that vast amounts of organic material created by plankton and other life settled on the seabed, experts say. That kind of carbon-rich buildup is needed to form oil.

Altogether, about six hundred vertical feet of the cores were rich, dark organic material, implying that there could easily be two vertical miles or more of similar organic layers in the deeper basins nearby, said Dr. Henk Brinkhuis, a geologist from Utrecht University in the Netherlands.

If sandstone and clay formed a lid over those layers, the deeper material could have cooked into oil or gas, he said. He stressed that this remained "crude speculation" until more surveying is done. But with demand for oil skyrocketing and known reserves dwindling, even the smallest hint is significant.

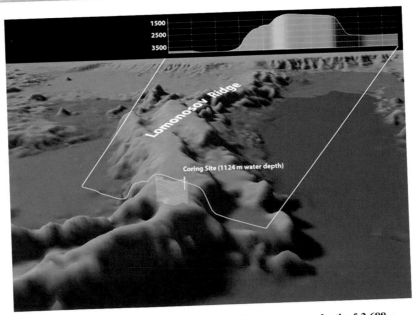

Core samples were taken from the Lomonosov Ridge at a water depth of 3,688 feet (1,124 meters).

A worker carries a drill bit that
will be used to extract samples
from the Arctic seabed.

Chapter Five

Glimpsing the
FUTURE

A crew member from one of the Russian helicopters is dancing on top of a heap of ice blocks that has formed where two great floating frozen plates collide. The grinding seam in the sea ice is just a hundred yards from the parked helicopters. The ice beneath the dancing man is chugging like an old steam locomotive building speed as it leaves a station. Every half minute or so, the little hill of ice slabs shifts slightly.

From about twenty yards away, I am watching this unnerving performance with Tim Stanton, a veteran Arctic oceanographer. Stanton is more interested in the ice than he is in the daredevil. "It's just amazing, isn't it?" he says, almost yelling to be heard over the huffing, squeaking sounds. "The pressures involved in these things are extraordinary." He says that the seams between some of these colliding plates can be sixty miles long.

Previous page: Dr. Timothy Stanton spent eighteen hours straight testing instruments suspended in the water through the sea ice beneath this yellow automated buoy.

The ice is moving under the influence of both winds and ocean currents. There are vibrations that we can sense through our feet. "You can feel the chunk that we're on actually starting to fail a bit," Stanton says, pointing to hairline cracks running here and there that I had not noticed until now.

"Does that mean we should back up?" I ask.

"Not yet," he says, smiling. "You can always jump over a crack."

Like many of the other scientists with me, Stanton lives for this ice world. Even when he is back at his home base, the Naval Postgraduate School in Monterey, California, he studies how sea ice affects the flow of heat between water and air. The work is a vital aspect of efforts to understand what may happen to the Arctic as the earth's climate warms. And there are few places on a warming earth as important to understand as the Arctic. In most parts of the planet, climate change is expected to be a gradual process, largely hidden by the normal wiggles of weather. Up here, however, a little warming can go a long way and actually trigger additional changes very quickly.

Basically, for most of the world, global warming from the buildup of greenhouse gases could unfold as if someone is slowly turning the knob on a thermostat. Here, the process could be more sudden and extreme, like flipping a switch.

There are two reasons that the Arctic may react strongly to climate change and possibly amplify it. They both relate to the ice beneath our feet. The first is that when blindingly brilliant white sea ice melts and is replaced by dark water, energy from the sun that would otherwise be reflected back into space is absorbed. Sea ice reflects more than 80 percent of the sun's energy. Open seawater absorbs more than 90 percent. So for every square mile of Arctic Ocean that changes from ice cover to open water in summer, far more energy from the twenty-four-hour sunshine gets in to warm the oceans. The laws of physics say that the absorbed heat will eventually seep back into the air, warming it.

The second reason the Arctic may act like a switch instead of a knob relates to the melting point of ice. As long as ice is below thirty-two degrees, it remains frozen. Temperatures can slowly rise from, say, fifteen degrees below zero to thirty-one degrees and a frozen vista like the Arctic Ocean will stay the same. But if the air temperature above the ice passes thirty-two degrees, then the ice begins to melt.

So to know what the future holds, which is the biggest and hardest question in climate science, researchers have to really understand the ice here—how it moves, how it reacts to changes in the water above and the sea below, and how it affects them in return.

Various surfaces reflect different amounts of sunlight. Some of the energy that is not reflected is absorbed in the form of heat, ultimately warming the planet.

Surface Reflectivity

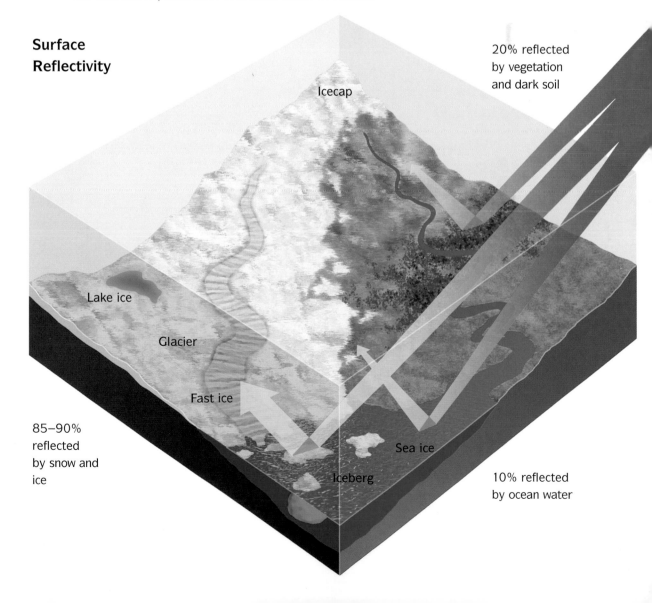

20% reflected by vegetation and dark soil

Icecap

Lake ice

Glacier

Fast ice

Sea ice

Iceberg

85–90% reflected by snow and ice

10% reflected by ocean water

Stanton has come along on this project to drill a hole in the ice and insert a $40,000 buoy that resembles a yellow, overgrown Tootsie Roll Pop. Its job is to provide a close-up view of the heat in the water just beneath the ice and in the ice itself. The long shaft is designed to stick through the hole into the sea and measure the salinity, or saltiness, of the water, its temperature, and currents that can move heat up, down, or sideways. Above the ice is a yellow dome containing a computer and disks that record the data. On top of that is a red and white crown with a satellite phone that will periodically dial Stanton's office back in California to send in the information it has collected.

Stanton has designed the buoy to withstand the same crushing pressures that are raising the ridge of ice beneath the reckless dancer.

But he knows that bad luck can still wreck such a device. In the second year of the North Pole observatory project, shortly after the team members left the ice and returned to their laboratories, they watched as the data transmitted from one buoy showed that it was being slowly tipped sideways. Then the data stopped flowing altogether. That could only mean that the buoy had been toppled and crushed by an ice ridge just like the one under the Russian dancer.

"There's no mechanical system you could really design to live through a thing like this," Stanton says, pointing as the greenish ice slabs rise and shift. "That's just the risk we take. It could last two days, it could last two years—you just don't know."

But it is worth trying, year after year, because each buoy that survives

Equipment and adventurers are scattered across the ice near the group of tents that serves as the North Pole Environmental Observatory.

will fill in one more gap in knowledge about the Arctic Ocean and climate.

And the gaps are still very large. The main method of figuring out what may happen here under the influence of accumulating greenhouse gases is to simulate the real world on powerful computers. Such simulations are an essential tool for climate research but remain, at best, a rough approximation of reality.

Most science progresses through experiments. If you want to see if a certain chemical harms plants, you grow some plants that are exposed to the chemical and some that are not, as a "control." With the puzzle of global warming, however, the experiment is being run on the whole planet as humans add more greenhouse gases to the air. There is no identical earth without the changing gases to use as a control.

Computer models are the next best thing. They simulate how heat, moisture, winds, currents, and clouds move and change in the atmosphere, and how much of the sun's warmth remains on earth or is bounced back to space, by dividing that incredibly complicated problem up into thousands of smaller ones. Everything that happens in the real atmosphere can be broken down into basic physics. The atmosphere and oceans are diced up into a grid of boxes, and computer programmers write sets of mathematical equations that reproduce the way energy or water vapor or other things flow from one to the next. The more powerful the computer, the more detailed the replica.

The ongoing explosion in the power of computers has allowed climate scientists to make their models ever more detailed and more like reality. But they are still limited, in the end, by those gaps in knowledge. When a weather forecast for a week from now—derived using similar computer models—fails, it is often because the model is missing information about the state of the atmosphere today.

For climate forecasts looking decades into the future, the challenges are even greater. The computer models do reasonably well at reflecting how the global climate responds to "forcings"—factors that can influence climate, like variations in the intensity of the sun or the insulating power of greenhouse gases. They also do a good job of replaying how the climate changed in the past. But they include approximations and educated guesses. When scientists use models to project how the Arctic climate and ice may change in a warming world, they include "error bars" in their graphs to show the level of uncertainty in their forecasts. They are always looking to other scientists to help them gain new knowledge about how the real world works so they can shrink those bars. That is where the people I am traveling with on the North Pole ice come into play.

When it is finally time for Tim Stanton to install his buoy, which he calls "my baby," all other distractions vanish. He hikes off to a spot on the ice that the Russian workers who first scraped the airplane runway said was particularly thick. His hope is that this broad, flat slab will last long enough to protect the buoy so it can keep transmitting data for many months as it is slowly carried across the Arctic Ocean.

It takes him ten hours to drill the hole and finally wrestle the probe into place. He attaches wires from the buoy to his laptop computer to start running what he calls "a farewell checkup."

And there is no sign of life. The buoy, which traveled five thousand miles on two bumpy airplane rides and was then hauled behind a bulldozer over the rough ice, might be dead. It is possible that a repair he made to a microchip a couple of days ago has failed.

He works with his laptop and a soldering gun and a screwdriver, often with no gloves on despite the cold. Eighteen hours after he began, he is finally done. The device is measuring heat. It is phoning home. In all that time, he has not even drunk a drop of water.

"These are show-stopper things I had to resolve sort of here and now," he says, after making his way to a tent and sipping some water another researcher produced by melting snow. "I couldn't say, Well, I'll sleep on it."

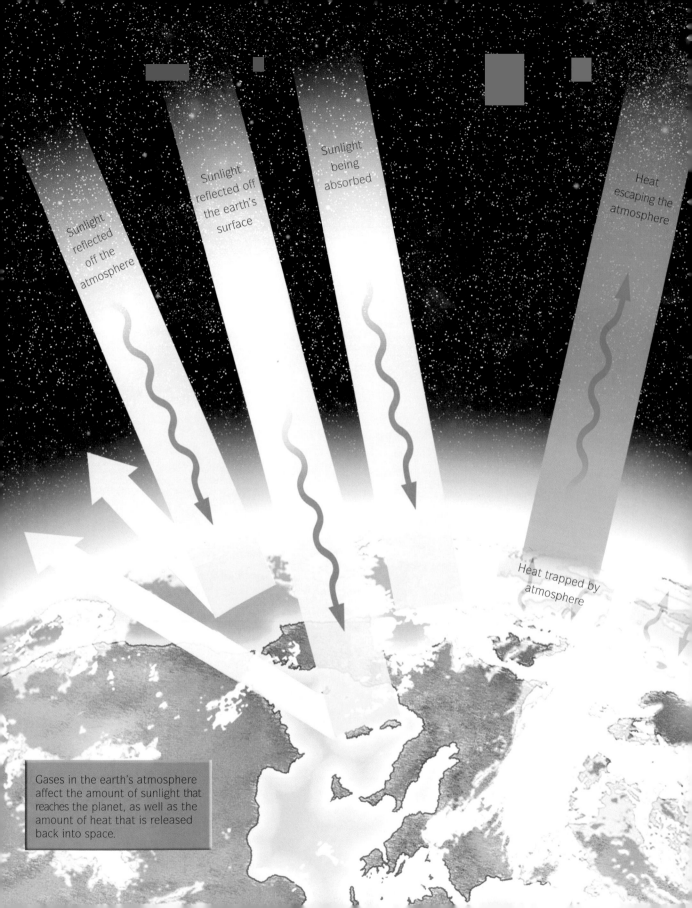

Sunlight reflected off the atmosphere

Sunlight reflected off the earth's surface

Sunlight being absorbed

Heat escaping the atmosphere

Heat trapped by atmosphere

Gases in the earth's atmosphere affect the amount of sunlight that reaches the planet, as well as the amount of heat that is released back into space.

From *The New York Times*

Who Cares About a Few Degrees?

BY ANDREW C. REVKIN

December 1, 1997: Scientists and other experts who have spent years trying to get people concerned about the prospect of global warming have always faced a central problem: temperatures change all the time. So why should anyone get excited about a global rise of a few degrees in a few decades?

But the issue is climate, not weather. Understanding the difference between the two is the first step in understanding why many scientists are predicting that changes that seem trivial in terms of any single day—a change, say, of five degrees Fahrenheit—could have a large impact on many facets of life when those changes are on a global scale.

Global warming would not change the range of weather experienced day to day, but it would increase the odds of having weather that is considered troublesome by twenty-first-century standards: summer droughts, winter deluges, and hurricanes and the like.

At the heart of global warming theory is the long-established idea that earth's atmosphere behaves like the roof of a greenhouse. In 1827 the French mathematician Jean-Baptiste Joseph Fourier recognized that the air circulating around the planet lets in sunlight, but prevents some of the resulting warmth from leaving. If the air had no heat-trapping effect, the heat from the sun would quickly radiate back into space, leaving the planet with a surface temperature of nearly zero degrees Fahrenheit.

In the 1850s, a British physicist, John Tyndall, took things further when he discovered that 99 percent of the atmosphere has no insulating properties at all. If the air did not contain carbon dioxide, the planet would be some twenty degrees cooler. Without water vapor, it would be a deep-frozen ball of ice.

Precise monitoring of carbon dioxide concentrations since the 1950s has shown a relentless upward trend. Some of the carbon dioxide has gone into the ocean, and some has been absorbed by growing trees, but the amount in the air has continued to rise.

There has been a simultaneous rise in the planet's average temperature, although at a far slower—and more uneven—pace. Other factors appear to have acted as a buffer, including a rise in the amount of sooty particles in the air; which reflect some of the sun's energy back into space before it can warm things up.

Nonetheless, many scientists, using computer models, say that they can account for buffering mechanisms and still see problems ahead, particularly if significant cuts are not made in the rates at which petroleum and coal are burned.

Even though the greenhouse gases exist in only trace amounts—they are measured in parts per million and, in some cases, parts per trillion—they exert a powerful influence on the temperature of the planet. So a tiny change in their concentrations can cause a big change in the way the atmosphere behaves.

From *The New York Times*

The Devil Is in the Details

BY ANDREW C. REVKIN

July 3, 2001: In 1922, Dr. Lewis Fry Richardson, a British physicist with a love for grand ideas, described how to forecast the behavior of the atmosphere.

He had details wrong but was correct in his basic concept: a series of equations that, when applied to measurements of heat, cloudiness, and humidity, could project how those factors would change over time.

There was one problem. To predict weather twenty-four hours in advance, he said, 64,000 people with adding machines would have to work nonstop—for twenty-four hours.

Dr. Richardson pined for a day "in the dim future" when it might be possible to calculate conditions faster than they evolved.

That dim future is now. But though much has changed, much remains the same.

Supercomputers have answered Dr. Richardson's plea. Weeklong weather forecasts are generally reliable. But long-term climate predictions are still limited by the range of processes that affect the earth's atmosphere, from the chemistry of the microscopic particles that form cloud droplets to the decades-long stirrings of the seas.

With its oceans, shifting clouds, volcanoes, and human emissions of heat-trapping gases and sun-blocking haze, earth remains a puzzle. According to Dr. Michael E. Schlesinger, who directs climate research at the University of Illinois at Urbana-Champaign, "If you were going to pick a planet to model, this is the last planet you would choose."

So even as the evidence grows that earth's climate is warming and that people are responsible for at least part of the change, the difficulty of the modeling problem is often cited by those who oppose international action to cut the emissions of heat-trapping gases.

Meteorologists track a storm using computer modeling.

High, thin clouds
absorb outgoing
heat.

**GREENHOUSE
GASES**, like
carbon dioxide
and methane, trap
heat.

**ATMOSPHERIC
CIRCULATION**

AEROSOLS
Ash, dust, smoke,
sea spray, water
vapor, sulfates, and
soot block incoming
sunlight.

**TERRESTRIAL
RADIATION**
Heat emitted by
the earth and its
atmosphere.

Convective clouds can
trap some heat but
also reflect it.

LAND COVER
Vegetation
absorbs carbon
dioxide and
sunlight, affecting
the land's reflectivity.

Locally,
mountains help
clouds develop.
Globally, they
affect circulations.

Low clouds block
solar radiation and
cool the earth.

**ICE SHEETS,
GLACIERS**

LAND LIFE

Wind pushes against
the ocean, creating
waves and currents.

**OCEAN–
ATMOSPHERE
EXCHANGE**

Deep currents transport
heat globally. Turbulence
mixes warm and cold
water locally.

SEA LIFE
Microscopic plants pull
carbon dioxide from the
atmosphere through
photosynthesis.

Weather and climate can be
affected by many different local
and global processes, which must
be included in accurate models.

Chapter Six

Three Broken
BOLTS

Six of the world's leading experts at solving Arctic riddles are on their knees on the sea ice thirty miles from the North Pole, stumped by three broken bolts. They are huddled around a broken electric winch next to a four-foot-wide hole that had been melted through the eight-foot-thick slab the day before.

Their pioneering, multimillion-dollar project to monitor the interactions between the atmosphere, ice, and sea here is paralyzed because one of the simplest pieces of equipment in their tons of gear has broken. A slender cable runs from the winch up to a tripod set over the hole and then straight down into the exposed slushy green water, which is sending up clouds of steamy "sea smoke," generated because the air is so much colder than the twenty-eight-degree water (salt water freezes at a colder temperature than fresh water). The mist from the hole and their exhaled breath builds frost on the men's whiskered faces.

Below the ice, the cable is attached to a string of instruments nearly two miles long that has been anchored to the seabed for a year, collecting irreplaceable information on how the ocean and ice behaved and changed through the course of twelve months. All year long, the

Previous page: A diver shoots film footage beneath the Arctic ice.

strand of instruments has been held vertically in the water—like a giant kelp frond—by big glass floats similar to those used in some ocean-fishing nets.

Everything has gone smoothly until now. Twenty-four hours ago, the scientists located the instruments by listening for a pinging sound produced by one of them. They dropped a small device through a hole and sent a special sound signal into the water that instructed a computer-controlled linkage between the anchor and the instrument chain to let go. Freed from the bottom, the instruments rose to the surface and bunched up under the sea ice, like a cluster of birthday balloons bouncing against a ceiling.

Some of the research in the Arctic Ocean takes place beneath the shifting cover of sea ice, requiring divers to descend into twenty-eight-degree water.

Two divers, Jim Osse and Eric Boget, slipped into special suits that keep them dry and relatively warm, strapped on air tanks and other

gear, and dropped down through that slushy opening, slowly descending into the frigid depths below. They each had a rope tether reeling out and back up to the surface for safety.

Osse told me later that descending beneath the polar ice is unlike anything else on earth. The water, which is free of silt, is as clear as the glassiest tropical lagoon. Sometimes you can see things three hundred feet away. "It's the closest thing I'll ever experience to being in outer space," he said. "You feel like this little guy out there in the vastness. That's what I was shaken by. Particularly if you drop down deep and really get the three-dimensionality of it all."

They swam about forty feet from the hole in the direction of the pinging, floating string of instruments and hooked it to the cable. All that was left was to activate the winch and draw the instruments up through the hole to retrieve the stored data and $200,000 worth of equipment.

That was yesterday. Now the whole project is in jeopardy because three bolts inside the winch have sheared off under the strain of tugging on the instrument chain.

Setbacks are normal in this kind of work. No one has ever made this kind of measurement at the top of the world. Until recently it would have been impossible to set instruments in the sea and return to find them. But with satellite navigation, the team can drop the equipment through a hole at a certain spot, fly back north a year later, and know exactly where to set up camp on the new sea ice to cut a fresh hole and retrieve their priceless data.

The ongoing project went well the first three years. Each time, the team lowered a chain of instruments with an anchor on one end and buoying floats on the other. A year later, the sound signal triggered the chain to let go of the anchor. Divers hooked the winch to the instruments. And the process was repeated. Not this time, however.

Without year-by-year data, it will be hard for scientists to figure out whether the big changes seen in the Arctic atmosphere and seas recently are some natural variation or related to global warming from human actions.

As with Tim Stanton's malfunctioning buoy, a fix has to be found. If not, the winch will be useless scrap, the instruments and last year's data will be stuck in the sea, and the new string of instruments for the coming year will sit uselessly on the ice near the team's tents.

As they work, Osse uses a sieve to scoop slushy "grease ice" out of the hole. If he does not clear the forming ice, the hole will quickly freeze shut. Such is the craft of science at the ends of the earth—particularly this end of the earth, where the pole sits over a fourteen-thousand-foot-deep ocean hidden by shifting ice. Unlike almost anywhere else on the planet, this environment requires a research team that combines the brainpower of scientists with the brute strength of furniture movers, the wile of small-town mechanics, the courage (or recklessness) of extreme athletes, and the willingness to carry a shotgun to ward off polar bears.

Hand-held navigation devices and satellite phones provide a welcome sense of connectedness. But in a place where the sea ice under your tent can suddenly crack, where help is at least five hundred miles away, even the simplest setback can threaten ambitious research and, potentially, the researchers themselves.

The winch crisis is just one of a pile of challenges, large and small, that have confronted these scientists as they have tried to make a routine out of research at the North Pole—which in the past was always an extraordinary one-time achievement.

They push ahead, knowing that without this effort, human understanding of the Arctic climate will be held back. Their work is improving understanding of the interactions of floating ice and air and water so that their colleagues who live in the world of theory back in warm offices and laboratories far away can look ahead with more confidence.

The measurements will help scientists understand what is contributing to the melting of the sea ice. Until now, a thin, shallow layer of fairly fresh, ultracold water has kept the ice from being exposed to much warmer, saltier water deeper in the sea. But the shallow cold layer has been getting thinner and thinner lately around the North Pole. If it gets much thinner, the ice can be melted from below as well as above. The only way to see if there is a trend is by measuring the ocean layers from top to bottom every year.

It is a continual work in progress, with problems and successes one year leading to changes the next. The project leader, Dr. Jamie Morison, said he would love to develop a permanent system for monitoring changes in the North Pole ice and the different currents flowing beneath it, mingling water from the Pacific, Atlantic, and the great rivers of Siberia and Canada.

A safety line ensures that a diver does not get carried away by currents under the ice.

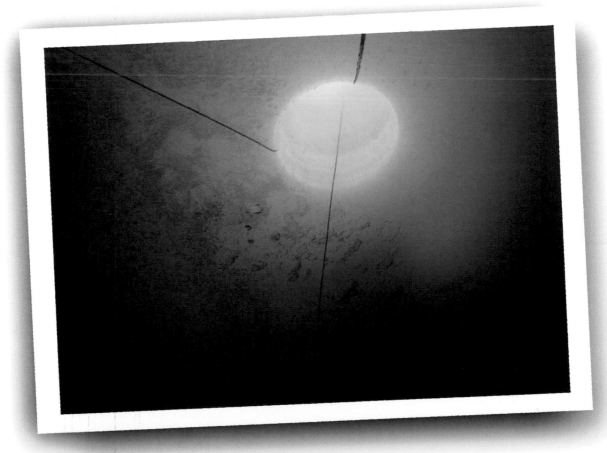

Scientist Jim Osse scoops ice from the surface of the water to prevent it from freezing solid.

When he is back at the University of Washington, Jim Osse designs underwater robots that can glide through the depths beneath sea ice, out of touch with the world, measuring ocean conditions day after day, week after week, and then return to open water to rise and send the information by satellite to scientists.

For the moment, though, there are no gliders under the North Pole ice. Success rides on finding replacements for three broken bolts. Time is running short. The Russian helicopter has been waiting for several hours to ferry some of the research team to the bigger base camp. There is no room for them to sleep here.

The pilot—with his fur hat made from the pelt of a wolverine that his copilot shot back in Siberia—is growing restless. Nobody knows how much longer he will wait. He has taken snapshots around the NORTH POLE WAS HERE sign, eaten some snacks, smoked some cigarettes.

Finally, tearing into another part of the winch, the scientists extract three bolts identical to the ones that were broken. They fit perfectly.

The rest of the winch is put back together.

Someone fires up the electrical generator that runs the winch motor. The pulley spins and the strand of instruments with that precious year of data begins to rise from the steaming, slushy hole.

A tiny new piece of the Arctic puzzle has been pulled from the depths.

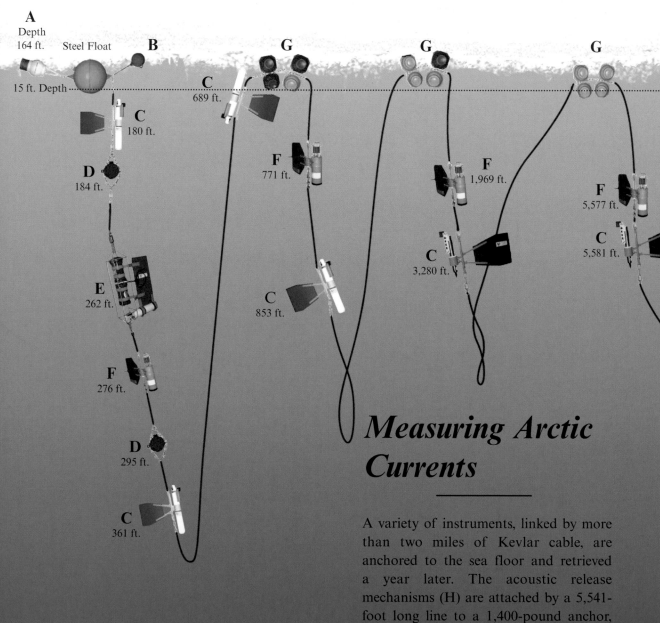

A
Depth
164 ft.   Steel Float

B

G

G

G

15 ft. Depth

C
689 ft.

C
180 ft.

D
184 ft.

E
262 ft.

F
276 ft.

D
295 ft.

C
361 ft.

F
771 ft.

C
853 ft.

F
1,969 ft.

C
3,280 ft.

F
5,577 ft.

C
5,581 ft.

Measuring Arctic Currents

A variety of instruments, linked by more than two miles of Kevlar cable, are anchored to the sea floor and retrieved a year later. The acoustic release mechanisms (H) are attached by a 5,541-foot long line to a 1,400-pound anchor,

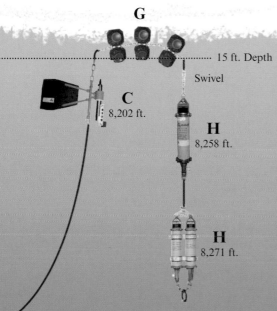

G

···· 15 ft. Depth

Swivel

C
8,202 ft.

H
8,258 ft.

H
8,271 ft.

positioning the line to float vertically in the water. When triggered by a radio signal, the acoustic releases disconnect from the anchor, allowing the instruments to float up under the ice in the position pictured here.

A. Upward-looking sonar measures ice thickness.

B. Recovery beacon sends signals to find the mooring when it is ready for retrieval.

C. Conductivity-temperature-depth recorders measure salinity and temperature.

D. Transponders serve as back-up beacons to help locate the chain as it floats under the ice.

E. Acoustic Doppler current profiler measures current characteristics.

F. Recording current meters measure the horizontal component of the current.

G. Floats bring the cable and instrument to the ice ceiling for retrieval after the anchor is detached.

H. Releases are triggered with a sound signal to free the mooring from the anchor. Anchor holds the chain in place at a sea floor depth of about 13,680 feet (2.6 miles).

From *The New York Times*

The constantly changing nature of the Arctic ice makes setting up research stations a risky business. In March 2004, the staff of an attempted year-round base was rescued after 90 percent of their station was swallowed by shifting ice.

Rescue on for Russian Crew

BY ANDREW C. REVKIN

March 5, 2004: Russia's first effort since the breakup of the Soviet Union to maintain a year-round presence on the sea ice near the North Pole was cut short yesterday after wind-driven floes rose into three-story ridges, destroying most of a drifting research camp.

Rough weather and warmer water at that position apparently conspired to shatter the broad plates of ice on which the camp and runway had been established, said Bernard Buigues, a French travel entrepreneur who works in partnership with Russian companies and the government on Arctic expeditions, adding, "The runways are broken and they have lost part of their equipment, but the lives of the people are not threatened."

The research station first developed troubles on Wednesday, when ice began shifting abruptly. A section of the half-square-mile floe holding the camp submerged, taking four of the station's six buildings with it.

"At 5:15 p.m. on Wednesday a huge wall of ice lumps reared up, initially three to five meters high, then seven to ten meters high," the base leader, Vladimir Koshelev, told Russia's First Channel. "In about half an hour, they swallowed up about 90 percent of the station. Such a thing, I would say, has never before been seen on a polar station. The wall immediately crushed under itself the accommodation and offices."

Knut Aagaard, an oceanographer at the University of Washington who has lived in such Arctic sea-ice camps more than twenty times since 1969, said rising ice ridges were less of a threat than the opposite phenomenon, the sudden opening of gaps.

"In the ridging events there's a tremendous variety of sounds," he said. "You just hurry up and pack up your stuff and move. The splits are the tricky ones. They're silent. You don't hear anything. You just wake up in the morning and look around and all of a sudden there's open water."

Members of the Russian research crew that was rescued after their camp was swallowed by the ice.

April 29, 2003 ●

Arctic Ocean

NORTH POLE

Line of Drift

As the Arctic ice drifts, it carries research stations with it. The Russian base had moved too far south, making it vulnerable to the effects of warmer temperatures.

March 2, 2004 ●

Greenland

Greenland Sea

Spitsbergen (Norway)

Chapter Seven

The Once and Future POLE

My three days on the North Pole ice are nearly done. The unheated Russian helicopter, crammed with gear and half-frozen members of the research team, roars into the air and heads back to Camp Borneo. Two men are remaining behind at the outpost, and the rest of us watch them, along with the steaming hole, winding winch, and tiny red tents, shrink and then disappear in a cloud of rotor-blown diamond dust.

As the big helicopter roars along, my brain spins from the strangeness and wonder of it all. For the last three days, we have been completely alone—we haven't seen even a bird in the blue sky. The only sign of life other than the scientists and trekkers and camp workers and pilots was a single seal that came up for a breath through one of the black openings in the ice. I had been crouched in one of my mesmerized moments, watching a ridge of heaped blocks of sea ice slowly build as two plates collided in slow motion. About fifty yards from me, a gray, whiskered face popped up from the rippling water. The small seal turned its head this way and that and watched me for a moment, just long enough for me to catch a grainy few seconds of it on my video camera. Then it slipped beneath the water and vanished.

Previous page:
A seal peers up
through a man-
made hole in the ice.

As I watched it, I was reminded of why all the scientists here keep a loaded shotgun at hand. Where there are seals, even here in the very middle of the Arctic Ocean, there are polar bears. These bears are some of the last animals on the planet that do not fear people—that see us as nothing more than a two-legged lunch. The thought made my neck prickle a bit, sitting there alone, half a mile from anyone else. And I kind of liked that. I liked the idea that this was a place where people could not yet feel comfortable. Humans have settled so many parts of the earth, from its deserts to the edges of this frozen ocean. They have climbed every mountain peak. The tallest, Mount Everest, was first conquered by two men in 1953, and in 2003—on the fiftieth anniversary of that climb—hundreds of amateur trekkers were clambering on its snowy shoulders to celebrate.

So to me it is reassuring to know that there is a place where, even

with all our technology, we cannot yet rest easy. We cannot even put up a flag or a stick marked NORTH POLE IS HERE without changing the IS to WAS because all the ice beneath us is on the move.

But now we may be conquering the pole in a different way, long distance. The Arctic already has been clearly affected by certain kinds of man-made pollution. Polar bears and traditional Inuit communities have some of the highest levels of industrial chemicals measured in the bodies of any living creatures on earth, even though they live far from any cities. This is because some toxic substances drift north on the wind and get absorbed by animals. These toxins do not break down inside the animals and instead wind up stored, mainly in the animals' fat. When smaller animals, such as fish, birds, and seals are eaten by larger ones (or humans), the substances are passed up the food chain, sometimes appearing in higher and higher concentrations in those toward the top.

Polar bears are fierce Arctic hunters. This one waited by a breathing hole for weeks in hopes of capturing a beluga whale. The whale pictured here escaped.

Now climate scientists are seeing more evidence that the retreat in Arctic ice and the warming air and permafrost are being caused at least partly by the buildup of heat-trapping gases released as humans burn coal and oil and cut down forests. Whether these gases flow from a taxicab in Boston or a power plant in Beijing, they are diffusing around the earth, holding in heat.

If the emissions continue to build and computer simulations are correct, the earth in summer will end up with a blue pole at the top and a white one at the bottom. That will be the most profound signal ever that humans have taken the reins of a planet. It would be a signal visible far into space that the earth has—to a significant extent—become what one species chooses to make it.

There could be some benefits of the warming, like open shipping lanes across the same sea where so many explorers perished as the ice closed in around their vessels. Growing seasons may lengthen and forests may shift north, although don't look for redwood groves on Ellesmere Island anytime soon. Oil and gas deposits that were untouchable beneath thick ice may be extracted as waterways open up. A Finnish company has already built two oil tankers for Arctic duty.

The ships have a rear end, or stern, built like an icebreaker. In thick sea ice, they travel in reverse, crunching through the floes like the ships in the core-drilling expedition in 2004. Once they reach open water, they simply turn around and travel like conventional tankers.

Already, countries with Arctic coastlines are waking up to the possibilities. Denmark and Canada are arguing over who owns certain islands around the Arctic Ocean—islands that until recently were meaningless lumps of ice-coated rock.

A dispute is brewing over that undersea mountain range running under the North Pole, the Lomonosov Ridge, where the drilling ship pulled up rock cores from fifty-seven million years ago. Denmark, which controls Greenland, is hoping to claim the ridge as an extension of its

Automobile exhaust contributes significantly to greenhouse gases in the atmosphere. Carpooling, driving more fuel-efficient cars, and using public transit can all help to reduce emissions.

territory under a complicated treaty called the Law of the Sea—and could thus claim control over the North Pole itself. Russia has already claimed half of the Arctic Ocean seabed as its territory, right up to the pole.

But there are also potential losses to consider in an unfrozen north. We may be remaking the Arctic so that in summertime there is no ice surface where the great white bears can stalk their seal meals, or Inuit hunters can do so, either. For the animal, that might mean a drift toward extinction. For the Arctic's ancient people, who have already been absorbing modern ways, it might mean an end to their traditions.

In the fall of 2004, the Inuit Circumpolar Conference, which represents more than 150,000 of the traditional peoples ringing the Arctic Ocean, announced that it planned to file a complaint with an international human rights commission against the United States for continuing to pump out greenhouse gases while knowing that those gases threaten a way of life.

Humans have always changed their environment, damming streams, planting crops, fencing pastures, netting fish. Much progress has happened this way. But in this century most climate experts have concluded that we are no longer just acting locally. In raising the capacity of the atmosphere to hold in the sun's energy, we have gone global.

As so many writers and thinkers have said, with power comes responsibility. Now, whether we like it or not, people are becoming responsible for the shape of things to come on earth. We are somewhat like a student driver, learning the rules as we roll along.

Scientists say that the great challenge with global, and Arctic, warming is that people need to make decisions now even though we don't yet understand all the rules and lack a clear road map. And it is unlikely to be clear anytime soon.

In 2000, for example, when scientists along on a tourist cruise to the North Pole reported seeing open water there, the result was a front-page headline in *The New York Times* and much discussion of whether the tipping point had been reached in a polar meltdown.

It quickly became evident that the situation was not nearly that simple. Sea ice builds and retreats in natural cycles that cannot yet be distinguished from any human influence on arctic conditions.

Uncertainty will long continue to cloud scientific projections of climate change, climate scientists say. Yet most experts also agree that if prompt actions are not taken to cut the rising flow of heat-trapping gases linked to warming, the odds will only mount that earth's climate could shift in truly profound ways later in this century.

The helicopter starts to rattle and shake as the pilot prepares to set us down at the ice station Borneo, where we will wait for our flight off the ice.

The camp has taken on the feel of a traveling circus, or maybe the bar scene in the original *Star Wars* movie that features an amazing assortment of aliens from across the galaxy. In the big pink and blue tent that serves as the camp cafeteria, several Moscow millionaires celebrate Russian Orthodox Easter by eating hard-boiled eggs, making toasts, and singing songs. They came here to parachute at the North Pole from helicopters.

A Finnish double-ended oil tanker that is specially designed for Arctic duty. One end functions like a regular tanker, while the other is shaped like an icebreaker, allowing the tanker to travel in reverse through thick ice.

Also celebrating are groups of British and Canadian ski trekkers who flew here to ski from Borneo to the pole and back (about one hundred twenty miles in all). They are frostbitten and unwashed and loud and happy and drinking vodka. They came for a little taste of the North Pole of old, the pole as a prize to gain at great peril.

A figure dressed in red flannel and white fur suddenly pops his head into the tent, looking for all the world like Santa Claus, although his red jacket is as long as a bathrobe and his hat is more like a wizard's. He is the Russian Father Christmas.

Then, an even stranger sight materializes. A beautiful Russian-speaking woman had arrived in camp with the wealthy Moscow skydivers. Everyone around me assumed she was just another parachutist. Now, though, Natalia Liberman sweeps out of her tent dressed in a floor-length (well, *ice*-length) white fur coat, a shimmering sequined gown, and a jeweled tiara in her long blond hair.

Liberman, it turns out, was the runner-up in a beauty contest. First prize was a

Top: Camp worker Yuri Petrovich, dressed as Father Christmas, dances with Natalia Liberman and an unidentified tourist.

Bottom: Workers disassemble the skeleton of a tent at Camp Borneo.

trip to the North Pole—but the winner turned it down. She poses for photographs with the Russian pilots, the ski trekkers, the scientists, even me.

After a while, it is time for the science team to get ready to depart. We pile our huge duffel bags full of extra gear onto the ice. It is time to wait, once again, for a helicopter ride to the ice runway to meet the airplane that will take us back to Canada.

I wander off for one last taste of Arctic silence and emptiness. Part of me does not want to leave, but I also know there is truth to a saying Jim Osse related to me: "In the Arctic, never pass up a meal, a shower, or a flight south."

Up here, you do not push your luck. Ice runways crack in half. In fact, the first one at the base camp this year had to be abandoned when it split in two not long after two Russian airplanes lifted off. An hour earlier, and those planes would have been marooned there until the ice melted and they dropped into the sea.

Away from the hubbub near the camp, I ignore my grandmother's advice and pull off my hood and facemask to feel the bite of the dry, icy air on my skin one more time and hear nothing but wind.

In a few weeks, this frozen realm will start to get slushy as the building heat of the sun, circling ever higher through the summer, eats away at the ice.

Before it is no longer possible to land an airplane, the Russians will fold up the tents and pack everything into a big Antonov cargo jet, and Borneo will disappear, just as if it were in fact a traveling circus.

I walk back to camp and help load our gear into the helicopter.

A few hours later, those who are leaving assemble at the runway, then clamber up the aluminum steps into the same twin-engine plane that brought us here what seems like ages ago.

The pilot wastes no time, knowing he has just enough fuel to come to the pole and get back. The engines roar. The diamond dust flies.

We circle over Borneo before flying south. The camp, which felt so loud and busy and full of people and their machines a little while ago, is now a dot on the endless white ice.

From *The New York Times*

As Polar Ice Turns to Water, Dreams of Treasure Abound

CHURCHILL, Manitoba, October 10, 2005: Pat Broe, a Denver entrepreneur, is no more to blame than anyone else for a meltdown at the top of the world that threatens Arctic mammals and ancient traditions.

Still, the newest study of the Arctic ice cap—finding that it faded this summer to its smallest size ever recorded—is beginning to make Mr. Broe look like a visionary for buying this derelict Hudson Bay port from the Canadian government in 1997. Especially at the price he paid: about $7. By Mr. Broe's calculations, Churchill could bring in as much as $100 million a year as a port on Arctic shipping lanes shorter by thousands of miles than routes to the south, and traffic would only increase as the retreat of ice in the region clears the way for a longer shipping season. With major companies and nations adopting a similar logic to Mr. Broe's, the Arctic is undergoing nothing less than a great rush for virgin territory and natural resources worth hundreds of billions of dollars.

All told, one quarter of the world's undiscovered oil and gas resources lies in the Arctic, according to the United States Geological Survey. Recent studies have projected that in a few decades there could be lucrative fishing grounds in waters that were largely untouched throughout human history.

Under a treaty called the United Nations Convention on the Law of the Sea, territory is determined by how far a nation's continental shelf extends into the sea. Claims of expanded territory are being pursued the world over, but the Arctic Ocean is where experts foresee the most conflict. Only there do the boundaries of five nations—Russia, Canada, Denmark, Norway, and the United States—converge, the way sections of an orange meet at the stem.

In 2001, Russia made the first move, staking out virtually half the Arctic Ocean, including the North Pole. But after challenges by other nations, including the United States, Russia sought to bolster its claim by sending a research ship north to gather more geographical data. On August 29, it reached the pole without the help of an icebreaker—the first ship ever to do so.

Denmark is particularly interested in proving that the Lomonosov Ridge is linked geologically to Greenland. If it finds such a link, Denmark could make a case that the North Pole belongs to the Danes, Danish officials have said.

Canada could also claim a huge area, and the United States could petition for a swath of Arctic seabed larger than California, according to rough estimates.

Canadian Forces Northern Area troops raise a Canadian flag on Hans Island, Nunavut.

An Inuit hunts the
old-fashioned way:
with a spear.

From *The New York Times*

A Changing World

BY CLIFFORD KRAUSS

September 6, 2002: At age eighty-five, Inusiq Nasalik has seen some changes in his day.

Born in an old whaling settlement, he lived in igloos and sod houses as a child and drove a dog team to hunt on the tundra through much of his life. Now he lives in a comfortable house with a plush sofa in his living room, a Westinghouse range and microwave oven in his modern kitchen, and a big stereo to play his favorite old Eskimo songs.

Life is good for him, he says, but he is worried about the changes he sees in the wildlife that surrounds this hamlet of Pangnirtung, Nunavut, on the shores of an icy glacier fjord just below the Arctic Circle.

He says the caribou are skinny, and so are the ringed seals, whose fur has become thin and patchy. The Arctic char that swim in local streams are covered with scratches, apparently from sharp rocks in waters that are becoming shallower because of climatic shifts. The beluga whales and seals do not come around the Pangnirtung fjord as much anymore, perhaps because increased motorboat traffic is making too much noise.

Hunters across the eastern Canadian Arctic are reporting that an increasing number of polar bears look emaciated, probably because their hunting season has been shortened by the shrinking ice cover.

Scientists say the problems Nasalik observes result from climate change and the gradual increase in contaminants. The people who eat such animals are also affected, and high levels of contaminants have been found in the breast milk of Eskimo women.

Nasalik and other local hunters and native elders are sharing their observations about changing wildlife with scientists who have come to appreciate their expertise at natural observation and long memories of environmental conditions in the Arctic. Researchers are beginning to teach Eskimos, better known as Inuit in Canada, how to collect scientific data and take measurements of hunted animals to detect everything from changes in the size of their organs to the abundance of their fat.

For Paulusie Veevee, seventy-five, an elder who started hunting with his grandfather when he was ten, the greatest tragedy of all is the changing habitat for the seals that depend on the ice for reproduction.

"The seals have their pups in dens on the ice," Veevee noted. "If there isn't enough ice, where will they have their babies—on land? That's the question I ask myself."

Paulusie Veevee (left) and Jonah Kilabuk take a bite of prepared whale skin and blubber, known as muktuk.

Source Notes

As a journalist, I try to start writing about something, whether it's the North Pole or the rain forest, based on what I know from my own experiences. But as a story or book grows, there are always spots where you can't rely on what you've seen yourself. That is when the research begins. You have to find people who are experts on particular aspects of an issue or event.

I spoke to many scientists who are studying the Arctic right now. These included specialists who know about the Arctic atmosphere, the sea ice, or the fish, mammals, and plankton living beneath it. Then there are the scientists who use computers to simulate how the atmosphere and ocean might behave in the future.

But those sources could not tell me about the past. That is the domain of historians and scientists who seek clues to the way the Arctic was before we had satellites and icebreakers to probe its secrets. I used the Internet to find many of the experts I needed, and then I went back to that old standard: books.

I have always loved books, especially dusty, yellowed ones. There are dozens of marvelous books, some very old and some recent, that describe the changing human relationship with this place called the North Pole. I was lucky enough to have a couple of them at home. My father had passed along to me one of the original books telling the conflicting stories of Frederick Cook and Robert Peary, the two men who first claimed to have reached the pole nearly a hundred years ago. I had it on my shelf long before I started focusing on the North Pole, or imagining that I might get there someday. Opening it was like bumping into a forgotten friend.

The other book I already had on hand was a study of the world's oceans written by the first American oceanographer, Matthew Fontaine Maury. My edition was published in 1859. I had gotten it while studying in London. It was in a heap of books being sold from a cart by a street vendor. Now it helped me learn about a time when even top scientists like Maury thought there was a warm open sea at the top of the world.

That is the wonderful thing about books. They capture not only facts, but the way people thought about the world at certain times. And that helps us understand a little bit about the way we are thinking about our world, in our time.

I also used several contemporary books and sources:

In Chapter 2, I learned about the ancient Hindu and Buddhist view of the North Pole from Chet Van Duzer's article, "The Mythology of the Northern Polar Regions: Inventio Fortunata and Buddhist Cosmology," in *At the Edge: Exploring New*

Interpretations of Past and Place in Archaeology, Folklore, and Mythology (March 1998): 8–16.

In Chapter 3, I found information on the expeditions of Lieutenant William Edward Parry in Charles Officer and Jake Page's *A Fabulous Kingdom: The Exploration of the Arctic* (Oxford University Press, 2001).

I'm also indebted to polar expert Dr. Stephanie Pfirman for her information regarding Fridtjof Nansen's expedition. It was she who pointed out that Nansen would "go with the floe."

And in Chapter 4, Karl Weyprecht's and Dr. E. Fred Root's quotes regarding the state of Arctic research in the nineteenth century were taken from "Antarctic Treaty System: An Assessment," *Polar Research Board of the National Academy of Sciences*, 1986.

The following articles from *The New York Times* appear as excerpts and illustrations:

1. Where All Is South
How to Get to the North Pole
Revkin, Andrew C. "Boots and Satellites." *Times Talk,* July 2003.

Reporting from the North Pole
Revkin, Andrew C. "Taking Technology to Extremes." *The New York Times*, June 5, 2003.

2. The Imagined Pole
Will Compasses Point South?
Broad, William J. "Will Compasses Point South?" *The New York Times*, July 13, 2004.

North Pole a Hole; Likewise the South
"North Pole a Hole; Likewise the South." *The New York Times*, April 4, 1908.

3. Cold Reality
Who Reached the North Pole First?
Leary, Warren E. "Who Reached North Pole First? Historian's Solutions." *The New York Times*, February 17, 1997.

Did Byrd Reach the North Pole?
Wilford, John Noble. "Did Byrd Reach Pole? His Diary Hints 'No.'" *The New York Times*, May 9, 1996.

4. The Polar Puzzle

Fiery Secrets in the Arctic Depths
Revkin, Andrew C. "Under the Arctic Ice, a Seabed Yields Some Fiery Secrets."
The New York Times, July 1, 2003.

Is There Oil Under All That Ice?
Revkin, Andrew C. "Under All That Ice, Maybe Oil." *The New York Times*,
November 30, 2004.

5. Glimpsing the Future

Who Cares About a Few Degrees?
Revkin, Andrew C. "Global Warming: Who Cares About a Few Degrees?"
The New York Times, December 1, 1997.

The Devil Is in the Details
Revkin, Andrew C. "The Devil Is in the Details." *The New York Times*, July 3, 2001.

6. Three Broken Bolts

Measuring Arctic Currents
Revkin, Andrew C. "Doing Science on Top of the World." *The New York Times*,
July 3, 2001.

Rescue on for Russian Crew
Revkin, Andrew C. "Rescue on for Russian Crew After Arctic Camp Collapses."
The New York Times, March 5, 2004.

7. The Once and Future Pole

Kraus, Clifford, Steven Lee Myers, Andrew C. Revkin, and Simon Romero. "As
Polar Ice Turns to Water, Dreams of Treasure Abound." *The New York Times*,
October 10, 2005.

A Changing World
Krauss, Clifford. "Pangnirtung Journal: Eskimos Fret as Climate Shifts and
Wildlife Changes." *The New York Times*, September 6, 2002.

Further Reading

For a more detailed look at the topics covered in this book, you may enjoy the following articles from the archives of *The New York Times*.

Amundsen, Roald, and his flight to the pole/dirigible travel at the pole
"How Zeppelin Plans to Try to Reach the North Pole by Airship."
The New York Times, July 26, 1909.

Owen, Russell D. "Amundsen Arrives at King's Bay Base."
The New York Times, April 22, 1926.

Ramm, Fredrik. "The Historic Message from the North Pole."
The New York Times, May 13, 1926.

Special Cable to the New York Times. "Shows Ice Pack at the Pole."
The New York Times, May 29, 1926.

Arctic wildlife and environment
Revkin, Andrew C. "Big Arctic Perils Seen in Warming."
The New York Times, October 30, 2004.

Revkin, Andrew C. "Hunt Imperils Polar Bears in Bering Sea, Report Says."
The New York Times, June 17, 2003.

Revkin, Andrew C. "Unfrozen North May Face Navy Blue Future."
The New York Times, January 13, 2004.

Sullivan, Walter. "The Changing Face of the Arctic."
The New York Times, October 19, 1958.

Byrd, Richard, and his flight to the pole/airplane travel at the pole
Browne, Malcolm W. "Ideas & Trends: Polar Heroes in History's Cold Eye."
The New York Times, May 12, 1996.

Witkin, Richard. "Airline Is Pioneering Polar Route in Los Angeles–Europe Run Today."
The New York Times, November 15, 1954.

Camp Borneo/Life at the North Pole
Revkin, Andrew C. "At the Bustling North Pole, Here Today, Gone Tomorrow."
The New York Times, April 28, 2003.

Revkin, Andrew C. "The World: Like Everest, the North Pole Draws a Crowd."
The New York Times, May 25, 2003.

Cold war activity at pole/the under-ice voyage of the USS *Nautilus*
"Arctic Defenses Urged: Two Air Colonels Declare Pole Is Likely Attack Route."
The New York Times, May 4, 1955.

Belair, Felix, Jr. "Nautilus Sails Under the Pole and 1,830 Miles of Arctic Ice Cap in Pacific-to-Atlantic Passage."
The New York Times, August 9, 1958.

Cook/Peary debate
"Berlin Is Skeptical."
The New York Times, September 2, 1909.

"Cook Reports He Has Found the North Pole."
The New York Times, September 2, 1909.

"Doubt Cast in London."
The New York Times, September 2, 1909.

"Newspapers Call It the Most Remarkable Coincidence in History."
The New York Times, September 7, 1909.

"Peary Discovers the North Pole After Eight Trials in 23 Years."
The New York Times, September 7, 1909.

Extreme sports at the North Pole
Revkin, Andrew C. "Briton Awaits Ride Home After Hike to Pole."
The New York Times, May 21, 2003.

Revkin, Andrew C. "Taking Technology to Extremes."
The New York Times, June 5, 2003.

Franklin, Sir John, Lady Franklin, and efforts to rescue the Franklin expedition
Gill, John Freeman. "Sun, Ice, and Explorers' Graves."
The New York Times, February 4, 2001.

"The Tragic History of Sir John Franklin: How He and All His Companions Vanished Forever in the Far North."
The New York Times, September 12, 1909.

"Told in an Arctic Diary: The Retreat from Fort Conger and Life on Cape Sabine."
The New York Times, December 3, 1891.

General history of North Pole exploration
"Pole the Goal of Centuries' Effort."
The New York Times, September 2, 1909.

Global warming
Revkin, Andrew C. "Ideas and Trends; Global Waffling: When Will We Be Sure?" *The New York Times*, September 10, 2000.
Revkin, Andrew C. "Some Big Ideas Wash Up One Bulb at a Time." *The New York Times*, December 8, 1998.

Sullivan, Walter. "Expert Says Arctic Ocean Will Soon Be an Open Sea." *The New York Times*, February 20, 1969.

Greely, Adolphus
Geographer, "Nature Near the Pole: Scenes and Phenomena of Arctic Life. The Scientific Observations of the Greely Party." *The New York Times*, August 18, 1884.

International debate over Arctic ownership
Krauss, Clifford. "Canada Reinforces Its Disputed Claims in the Arctic." *The New York Times*, August 29, 2004.

Inuit life and culture
Revkin, Andrew C. "Eskimos Seek to Recast Global Warming as a Rights Issue." *The New York Times*, December 15, 2004.

Kane, Elisha Kent, and the open polar sea
"The New Arctic Expedition." *The New York Times*, January 31, 1853.

Plaisted, Ralph
"4 Men, in a 44-Day Trek, Reach the North Pole in Snowmobiles." *The New York Times*, April 20, 1968.

Vecsey, George. "Snowmobile Conquerors of North Pole Looking for Adventure Southward." *The New York Times*, January 26, 1969.

Research and technology at the North Pole
Revkin, Andrew C. "Doing Science at the Top of the World." *The New York Times*, May 13, 2003.

Revkin, Andrew C. "On the Sea Ice 30 Miles from the North Pole." *The New York Times*, May 13, 2003.

Sullivan, Walter. "In the World Beneath the Ice." *The New York Times*, March 12, 1972.

Weyprecht, Karl, and the International Polar Year/International Geophysical Year
Geographer. "The Greenland Colony: Projects for Polar Exploration." *The New York Times*, March 3, 1877.

Sullivan, Walter. "34 Adrift on Arctic Ice for Scientific Studies; Americans Living on Ocean Get Data for Geophysical Year." *The New York Times*, June 9, 1957.

Internet Resources

The following Web sites provide an excellent starting point for Internet reading on North Pole history and research:

Amap.no/acia/
The Arctic Climate Impact Assessment Web page. Reports the findings of a study commissioned by the Arctic Council, an international organization comprising eight nations with Arctic territory. This is the most thorough review of changing conditions around the North Pole.

Psc.apl.Washington.edu
Web site of the North Pole Environmental Observatory.

pearyhenson.org
Home of the Peary & Henson Foundation on the Web.

www.apl.washington.edu
The wizards at the University of Washington who make instruments for collecting data at the North Pole.

www.arcus.org
The Arctic Research Council of the United States. This site tracks most Arctic research involving American scientists and includes additional links on Arctic themes.

www.cookpolar.org
Official Web site of the Frederick A. Cook society.

www.IPY.org
Web site of the 2007–8 International Polar Year.

www.rcom-bremen.de/English/Summary.html
Web site of the Arctic Ocean Coring Expedition of 2004, which recovered the first long-term record of ice and climate changes from the central Arctic Ocean.

www.thepoles.com
This Web site tracks expeditions to the North Pole and Antarctica, with detailed day-by-day accounts of extreme explorers.

Acknowledgments

The narrative at the heart of this book only exists because many people helped me in many ways. They included the scientists and support staff who allowed me to accompany them north and spent precious time explaining their work instead of simply doing it. I owe a particular debt to Dr. Jamie Morison from the University of Washington, the leader of the North Pole Environmental Observatory project, not just because he had the foresight to make that salmon sandwich that, despite freezing, got a few of us through a very long day. And I could not have gone to the top of the world without the assistance of the National Science Foundation's Office of Polar Programs, and especially Peter West, who helps journalists do their jobs at both poles.

There would have been no book, as well, without the support of Cornelia Dean and Laura Chang, the two science editors of *The New York Times* I've worked under while doing my Arctic reporting. They both recognized the importance of the big changes under way at the furthest ends of the earth and essentially cut my leash, letting me roam the unfreezing north three times in two years.

My editor at Kingfisher, Deirdre Langeland, was an indispensable guide to what for me is a new and very special universe, writing for younger readers. I'm convinced there is no more important audience, particularly when writing on the global environment, which is something that belongs to all generations at once. I also thank Nancy Grant at Kingfisher and Alex Ward, the director of *The Times*'s book efforts, for seeing the value of a tale about the changing North Pole.

Dr. Stephanie Pfirman, an all-around expert on the Arctic and chair of the Department of Environmental Science at Barnard College, provided great feedback and helped me avoid a couple of errors. Any that remain are my responsibility alone.

No one is owed more gratitude than my sons, Jack and Daniel, and my wife, Lisa Mechaley, who is a gifted middle-school science teacher and naturalist. They not only coped with my absences and static-filled satellite-phone calls but also offered a vital sounding board for my ideas as the book took shape.

Finally, my Arctic story is built on shelf upon shelf of essential volumes, articles, and research papers written by others who ventured north long before I did, in far more daunting conditions.

My insulated hat is off to all of them.

Picture Credits

The publisher would like to thank the following for permission to reproduce their material. Every care has been taken to trace copyright holders. However, if there have been unintentional omissions or failure to trace copyright holders, we apologize and will, if informed, endeavor to make corrections in any future edition.

Cover: Peter West/NSF; pages 1: Peter West/NSF; 2–3: Andrew Revkin; 7: Peter West/NSF; 8–9: Gordon Wiltsie/NGS/Getty Images; 10–11: Peter West/NSF; 12–13: Andrew Revkin (left), Ronald Verrall (background); 14–15: Andrew Revkin; 16–17: NASA; 18: Andrew Revkin; 20: Peter West/NSF (top), Andrew Revkin; 21 & 22: Andrew Revkin; 23 Peter West/NSF; 24–25 Paul Nicklin/NGS/Getty Images; 26–27: National Library of Canada (left and center) (nlc000703-v6 and nlc000701-v6); National Archives of Canada (nmc-0021063); 28–29: National Maritime Museum, London (top); 30–31: National Maritime Museum, London; 32: Collection of the Glenbow Museum, Calgary, Canada (phn-9850); 34: Paul Nicklin/NGS/Getty Images; 35: Mary Evans Picture Library; 36–37: National Maritime Museum, London; 38–39: National Maritime Museum, London; 42: National Library of Canada (nlc000885), 43: National Archives of Canada (C-001352); 45: US Naval Academy Museum, Annapolis, MD; 46: Library of Congress/Prints & Photographs Division; 49: Library of Congress/Prints & Photographs Division; 50–51: Times Wide World; 50: UPI; 51: Bettmann/Corbis, 52–53: Arctic Submarine Laboratory/US Navy; 54: Bettmann/Corbis; 56: Corbis; 57: Times Wide World; 58–59: Andrew Revkin; 60: Greg Probst/Corbis; 62–63: NOAA/from Vol.1, Annales of the International Geophysical Year; 65: US Naval Historical Center; 67: Hannes von der Fecht/ACEX; 68: M. Fagg/Australian National Botanical Gardens; 69: Dr. Henk Brinkhuis; 71: Hannes von der Fecht/ACEX; 72: NOAA; 74: M. Jacobsson/IDOP; 75: Hannes von der Fecht/ACEX; 76–77: Peter West/NSF; 80–81: Peter West/NSF; 86: Jim Reed/Science Photo Library; 88–89: Doug Allen/Nature Picture Library; 90: James Johnson/Polar Science Center/University of Washington; 92–93: Paul Aguilar/Polar Science Center/University of Washington; 95: Peter West/NSF; 98: AFP/Getty Images; 100–101: Galen Rowell/Corbis; 102–3: Sue Flood/Nature Picture Library; 104: Robyn Beck/AFP/Getty Images; 107: Fortum Shipping, Finland; 108: Andrew Revkin (top); Tim Stanton/NPS; 111: Canadian Department of National Defense; 112: Robert Galbraith; 113: Robert Galbraith; 114: Ronald Verrall; 115 Andrew Revkin; 116–17: Peter West; 118–20: Andrew Revkin; 121: Peter West/NSF; 122–26: Peter West/NSF

Index

Page numbers in **bold** refer to illustrations.

Measurements in this book appear in U.S. customary units. You can convert these units of length, distance, weight, and temperature by using the following conversion instructions.

Temperature

Fahrenheit to Celsius..........subtract 32, multiply by 5, and divide by 9

Length

inches to millimeters..........multiply by 25.40

inches to centimeters.........multiply by 2.54

feet to centimeters............multiply by 30.48

yards to meters................multiply by 0.9144

miles to kilometers...........multiply by 1.6093

Mass

ounces to grams...............multiply by 28.349

pounds to kilograms..........multiply by 0.4536